ANY IDEAS?

*"If you want to have good ideas
you must have many ideas."*

Linus Pauling, Nobel Prize-winner for Chemistry

Rob Eastaway

ANY IDEAS?

Tips and Techniques to Help You
Think Creatively

WATKINS

Sharing Wisdom Since
1893

First published in 2007 under the title *Out of the Box*
This extensively revised edition first published in the UK and USA 2017 by
Watkins, an imprint of Watkins Media Limited
19 Cecil Court
London WC2N 4EZ

enquiries@watkinspublishing.com

1 3 5 7 9 10 8 6 4 2

Illustrations by Bonnie Dain for Lilla Rogers Studio and Jade Wheaton

Typeset by Clare Thorpe

Printed and bound in Finland

A CIP record for this book is available from the British Library

ISBN: 978-1-78678-021-8

www.watkinspublishing.com

CONTENTS

INTRODUCTION

Everyone needs ideas.

Maybe they are just ideas for something routine, like thinking of a birthday present, or deciding what to do this weekend.

But there are times when you need to come up with ideas for more important things: ideas for a speech or a big presentation at work; how to decorate your house on a budget; how to balance your family and work commitments; or even – for more and more people these days – coming up with an idea for a new product or business.

Of course, ideas are needed to solve problems too: when you're stuck, sometimes the only way forward is by thinking around the problem with what's often called lateral thinking.

Without ideas you can't be creative, and in a world that is constantly changing, where it's becoming rare to find jobs in which you can spend years following a routine, we're all being forced to become more creative whether we like it or not.

This is a book about how to have ideas, on your own or in collaboration with others, and how to nurture them so they help you to solve everyday problems.

Ideas do, of course, happen by themselves, they are a natural part of how the human brain works.

But sometimes they need a helping hand, so there are tips here about techniques that can significantly increase the number of ideas that you have.

Creative thinking can help you to come up with better solutions to problems. It can also lead you to new experiences and opportunities that just make life a bit more exciting and fun. And that's what most of us want.

IDEA-KILLING

Unfortunately, ideas have enemies. Idea-killers.

Ideas can be fragile things, and it doesn't take much to kill them off. Ideas are often killed off just by being ignored, but they can also be killed by being criticized or laughed at.

There are two main idea-killers. These are:

OTHER PEOPLE

and

YOU

If you want to have more good ideas in life, then it's vital to be able to recognize idea-killers so that you can protect yourself against them.

Idea-killing (and how to avoid it) is a recurring theme in this book. It's discussed in Chapter 2 (about personal blocks), Chapter 5 (Exchanging Ideas) and Chapter 8 (Holding Ideas Meetings) and Chapter 10 (Brainstorming).

When trying to overcome idea-killing, there is one principle that is so important it also deserves a mention up front – and that is that you need to nurture and protect silliness.

THE IMPORTANCE OF SILLINESS

Not all ideas seem sensible when they are first aired. In fact, if an idea is genuinely novel, then by definition it is something that hasn't been encountered before; and when we haven't seen something before, we are, as human beings, naturally sceptical. "Oh you couldn't do that …", "Oh that would never work …".

This means that many new ideas will at first seem a bit … silly.

And of course not all silly ideas are good ones, many deserve to be killed immediately. But among them are some that don't. It's often the ideas that at first seem silly and impractical which turn out to be the best.

About 20 years ago, somebody somewhere made a suggestion: "At stores, instead of having to have your groceries scanned by a checkout operator, why not arrange it so that you scan all the items yourself." That person could easily have been laughed out of the room. "The supermarket would be bankrupt in a week!" Instead, that idea got picked up, and these days self-scanning is normal practice (even if it isn't universally popular).

Other ideas that would no doubt have been dismissed as fanciful, impossible or just downright silly just 20 years ago include:

- A taxi service where the drivers don't know their way around the city (Uber).
- Injecting a deadly toxin into your face to make you look younger (Botox).
- A TV show where you watch people watching TV (*Gogglebox*).
- A device that allows you to print sophisticated solid objects (3D printers).

And the list goes on.

So as you read through this book, remember that if you want to have more ideas, there are times when you need to allow yourself to be just a little bit more silly – if not in the things that you do, at least in the things that you think.

AH, AHA AND HAHA

This book is the result of an idea. I first had that idea (to write a book about creative thinking) 20 years ago. The first version was binned after a couple of months, and there were several years when the idea was left on the shelf, then there was a first attempt (under the title *Out of the Box* and written to somebody else's brief) in 2007, before it finally ended up as the book you are now reading. Like many ideas, it only turned into this finished product after several iterations and dead ends.

Why did I want to write this book?

For as long as I can remember, I've been interested in puzzles.

I always particularly enjoyed puzzles that involved "Aha!" moments. In my junior school I had a teacher, Mr Hudson, who used to like posing us questions like this:

Tom lives on the 20th floor of a block of flats. One Monday morning, Tom gets in the lift, rides down to the ground floor and heads out. When he returns later that day he presses the button for the 16th floor, gets out and walks up the final four flights of stairs to get to his flat. Why doesn't Tom take the lift all the way up to the 20th floor?

There could have been lots of reasons why Tom made the detour. The point of these so-called lateral-thinking puzzles is to figure out what happened by asking questions.

"Was the lift working properly?"
"Yes."
"Did Tom want to get out at the 16th floor to do something?"
"No, he wanted to go the 20th floor."
"Was something blocking the lift exit?"
"No."

The solution? It turns out that Tom was a young boy on his way to school. He could reach the button for the ground floor, but he wasn't tall enough to reach button 20 when he returned. The highest button he could reach was 16 so he pressed that and had to walk up the rest.

The "Aha!" feeling when you solve a puzzle like this is closely related to creative thinking. In the 1950s, the philosopher Arthur Koestler wrote a book called *The Act of Creation*, in which he proposed that creativity is Art, Discovery or Humour. Somebody else summed this up as: "Ah, Aha and Haha".

My interest in "Aha!" puzzles stuck with me, and for a few years I became a monthly puzzle-setter for *New Scientist* magazine. It was an exciting but sometimes nerve-wracking immersion into a world where I had to come up with something new every month. And it had to be an idea that worked: a puzzle that had a flaw and couldn't be solved was worthless, as I discovered when my second *New Scientist* puzzle proved to be a dud, prompting dozens of letters from angry readers. Setting puzzles to a deadline was excellent training in practical creativity.

That involvement with puzzles got me interested in creative problem-solving techniques, and for several years I ran workshops on this topic for civil servants and graphic designers. It is also what led me to start writing books about the hidden maths of everyday life.

Puzzles and maths in turn have led to me running Maths Inspiration, interactive maths lecture shows for teenagers held in theatres around the UK. Producing stage shows is fertile ground for creative ideas: every year we have to come up with new ideas for material and ways of presenting to ensure we keep audiences engaged. "What if we get the audience to do a Mexican wave …?"; "How about getting two volunteers to build a tower onstage using tin cans ...?"

So, while I'm fascinated in the whole process of how ideas happen, I'm just as interested in how to make them work.

This book is tips and techniques for having and acting on ideas in everyday life, either alone or with other people.

But its origins were in the "Aha!" moments of puzzle-solving.

"Why, sometimes I've believed as many as six impossible things before breakfast."

The White Queen, *Through The Looking Glass*

READING THIS BOOK

This is a book you can read from start to finish, but it's also one you can just dip into. The book has two main sections: Chapters 1–4 are about the process of having ideas *on your own*. Chapters 5–10 are about having ideas *with other people* – both one-to-one exchanges and in meetings. (Chapters 11–12 apply to both.)

Although many of the techniques lend themselves to the workplace, most of the principles are universal. For example, one extremely useful tool for developing ideas is a whiteboard, something that is normally found in an office or a school. Most homes don't have a whiteboard on the wall – but there's one in my kitchen, and I can vouch that it has been a constant focus of creative output for my family.

Dotted through the book you will find puzzles, exercises and other asides (solutions to puzzles can be found at the end of the book). There are also four famous examples of **Messy Creativity**. Creativity is often seen as a flash of inspiration that leads to a brilliant result. What we rarely see is the messy process by which many inventions and creations come about – the blind alleys, arguments and hopeless prototypes. The examples of messy creativity are a reminder of how wonderfully random and unstructured the idea process can be.

THANK YOUS

Thank you Alison Kiddle, Jill Walsh, Timandra Harkness, Dave Birch and my wife Elaine Standish, who not only had plenty of ideas to offer but were also there as sounding boards when I needed them most. Thank you to the Twitter community, who were, as ever, a rich source of material when I asked for suggestions, and to Dennis Sherwood for some lovely examples of opposites.

Thanks to Jo Lal for being such an easy-going and receptive publisher, which made the creative process so much easier. And special thanks to my friend Ben Sparks who suggested "Any Ideas?" as a title when we were having an informal brainstorm over a cup of coffee. We (and the publisher) came up with numerous ideas for titles, but it's *Any Ideas?* that I liked most. So that's why this book isn't called *Ignite Your Creative Spark* or *Beyond the Blue Sky* or *What's The Big Idea?* As Linus Pauling said, in order to have a good idea you need to have lots of ideas.

1
IDEAS AND WHERE THEY COME FROM

An idea is a thought about something that might be done or created.

"Why don't we go to the beach?" is an idea. So are "What if I start my talk with that joke about the cheesegrater?" or "How about a tune that starts 'do-doo bah doo-bah'."

Ideas can be good or bad, new or old. We'll come on to judging the quality of ideas later. The important point is that you are having ideas all the time, but many of them are so short lived and subconscious that you are barely aware of them.

HAVING IDEAS

Let's explore what it feels like when you try to have ideas.

ONE-MINUTE CHALLENGE: THE INKLESS BALLPOINT PEN

For this exercise you will need something to record your ideas – a smartphone, or a pencil, paper and a timer. Find them now before you start!

Ready?

OK, imagine that you've just been presented with a cheap ballpoint pen, made out of clear plastic. The pen has one big drawback: it has run out of ink.

Give yourself ONE MINUTE to record as many things as you can think of that you can do with the inkless pen.

Start ... now.

OK, how did you do in the one minute challenge?

- Most people find this exercise difficult, and come up with no more than three ideas. The most common idea of all is: "Throw the pen away and forget about it."
- Some people think of four or five ideas. Typically, these will be practical ways in which they've used a defunct ballpoint pen in the past – for example, as a pointer, or for punching a hole.
- A few people score much higher. I've known the odd individual score as high as fifteen ideas in a minute.

You can see some of the different uses to which people have put the inkless pen on page 144, and this is just the start. Many of those ideas may seem weak, but others may strike you as quite clever and creative.

It shows that there are plenty of ideas out there as long as we aren't worried about quality. Given time, between us we could probably find as many as a thousand ideas for using a defunct ballpoint pen.

There are all sorts of reasons why you might have come up with so few ideas. We'll explore those barriers to being creative in the next chapter.

But first, let's explore where ideas come from.

WHERE DO IDEAS COME FROM?

What is it that causes an idea to pop into your head? Here's where ideas typically come from:

PAST EXPERIENCE

We draw very heavily on what we've experienced before. Suppose you're having to think up ways to fundraise for a charity. The first ideas you have will almost certainly be ones that you have come across in the past – a sponsored bake-off or running a marathon, for example. So the more diverse your past experiences have been, the bigger the pool of ideas you have to draw from.

NECESSITY – THE MOTHER OF INVENTION

Do you know how to build your own home and live off the land? If you suddenly found yourself stuck on a desert island, you'd have no choice but to learn. Ideas flow when you need them, so facing – or even creating – a problem that needs solving is one way of ensuring that you come up with ideas.

BEING FED UP WITH HOW THINGS ARE

Feeling dissatisfied with a situation is a strong trigger for ideas. In 19th-century London, open sewers discharging into the Thames made many areas smell foul. But the politicians were not personally affected so they weren't motivated to come up with ideas to fix it. This changed in 1858 when the smell from the Thames became so noxious ("The Big Stink") that the Houses of Parliament closed. Suddenly everyone had ideas on how to solve the problem. The result was the sewerage system that survives to this day.

SEEING SOMEBODY ELSE'S IDEA

Ideas spread through communities like a virus. If one trendsetter starts taking selfies, suddenly everyone wants to. Then somebody thinks, "Wouldn't it be handy if there was something to hold the camera", and the trend of the selfie stick is born. The more you see of how other people come up with ideas or solve problems, the more ideas you're likely to find for your own situation.

BEING "RIPE"

Sources for ideas are all around us, but for those ideas to leap out, we often need to be in a state of mind that the philosopher Arthur Koestler described as "ripe". He noted that the more immersed people were in a problem, the more likely it was that they would be ripe for having ideas.

A TANGLED PROBLEM

In the 1940s, Swiss engineer George de Mestrel started wondering how to create a better way to fasten clothing after the zip fastener on his wife's dress got stuck one day. Months later, when out walking in the mountains, he spotted burrs clinging to his dog's coat. The burrs turned out to have tiny hooks, which were snagging on loops of the dog's hair.

Because de Mestrel's mind was ripe for an idea about fasteners, at that moment he came up with the hook-and-loop concept behind Velcro.

PUZZLE: AS EASY AS ABC?

Here's a puzzle for which (unusually for puzzles) there is no such thing as a wrong answer. Whatever answer you come up with will be fine.

If ABC goes to ABD then what does XYZ go to?

Think of an answer (any answer!) now, before you read ahead.[1]

FAMILIAR PATTERNS

You might be surprised how much the ideas you have are influenced by patterns you have encountered before.

If your answer to the puzzle above was XYA, you thought the same way as about 70 per cent of adults that I've given this puzzle to.

Why is it that most people come up with XYA as their answer?

It's to do with a pattern that we're all used to, where things go in cycles. When a clock gets to 12, it goes back

---

1 This question was first posed by Douglas Hofstadter.

to 1 again. Many people apply this same cyclic pattern to letters: since Z is the last letter, then why not go back to A and start again? There's nothing wrong with this answer, but it's not the only one you could have come up with.

Here are some other answers that people offer:

XY1

XY

XYD

WYZ

XYAA

Some of these answers might strike you as creative. The person who suggested XY1 felt that after the letters come the numbers. The XY person reckoned that since nothing follows Z, it should be a blank, while XYD decided that the rule was "always replace the last letter with D". The person who said WYZ thought that if the right-hand letter Z is unable to move "outwards", then the left-hand letter, X, must bounce "inwards" instead to become W.

And what about the answer XYAA? How did this mould-breaking person come up with the idea of adding a fourth letter?

As it happens, the woman who gave me the answer XYAA is an accountant, and she thought it was "obvious". She uses a spreadsheet every day, and the column after Z in a spreadsheet is AA. When I asked her what she thought about the answer XYA instead, she said, "Oh, I do like that – who thought of that one?"

You may not have thought of her idea, but then, nor would she have thought of yours. New ideas sometimes depend simply on having a different experience. The example of XYAA shows that when it comes to having ideas, two heads can be much better than one.

IDEA PEOPLE

Ideas will come to anybody, but there's no doubt that they come more easily to some people than to others. We can all probably think of individuals that we would describe as "Idea people" – creative thinkers who seem to come up with more ideas than we do.

But no two creative thinkers are the same. If you now try to think of acquaintances who are good with ideas, they probably have quite different attributes from each other. Here are some people I know who I think of as Idea people (I have changed their names to protect their modesty):

JOE – A BUILDER

When you ask Joe to take on a project, he is quick to come up with several options from the start. "We could do this … or we could do this …" Faced with an unexpected problem he never gets stuck for long and always seems to find a neat and elegant way around it.

LAURIE – A PR EXECUTIVE

Laurie looks at the world in a different way from most people and finds angles that are unconventional, but (usually) work. She also has a dry, quick sense of humour, which can be great for sparking new ideas. "Why don't we …?"

SIMON – A COMPOSER
As well as composing music, Simon is a great enthusiast about life. Tell him about a new idea, and he'll invariably be excited and see the possibilities. "I love that … it reminds me of …"

KELLY – A COOK (IN HER SPARE TIME)
Give Kelly a brief and she'll create what you want – but with clever extras. She's a perfectionist, driven to keep refining her ideas right to the end. "I'm going to add this …", "I'm not happy with that, I think we could do this instead …"

DIFFERENT CREATIVE QUALITIES
Each person in the list above has a combination of skill and outlook that makes him or her good at what they do. There are particular traits that go with creativity. A creative thinker might be someone who:
- Is a bit eccentric and approaches things at a different angle from everyone else.
- Challenges everything.
- Builds on your ideas rather than knocking them.
- Is driven by a desire to create things.
- Is never stopped by a problem for long.
- Sees connections between apparently unrelated topics.
- Fine-tunes ideas until they work perfectly.

However, it's unusual for anyone to have all these attributes in all situations. If Joe and Laurie swapped jobs, their creative side might not show at all.

Is it possible to turn yourself into more of an Ideas Person? To some extent, yes. The techniques described in Chapters 4, 6, 7 and 11 are some of the ways to do this – and while these might feel fake to begin with, after a while it becomes hard to tell the difference between fake creativity and the real thing.

One other way to gently nudge yourself to becoming a creative thinker is to change the language you use.

THE LANGUAGE OF IDEAS

It could be said that creative thinkers are one of five types: the child-like thinker, the problem-solver, the dreamer, the builder and the "imagineer". Each type can be summed up with a pair of words – Why not? How to ..., I wish ..., Yes and ..., and What if?

The path to being more open to ideas, and having more ideas yourself, can be as simple as uttering one of those pairs of words. "Why not ... try a new route to work this week?" "I wish ... I could write a novel."

"Everyone is a genius at least once a year. The real geniuses simply have their bright ideas closer together."

Georg Christoph Lichtenberg, physicist

TYPE	CHARACTERISTICS	WORDS
Child-like	Has the curiosity and confidence to explore ideas.	"Why not?"
Problem-solver	Regards every setback or block as a problem to be solved.	"How to ..."
Dreamer	Aspires to what might be, rather than what is.	"I wish ..."
Builder	Supports other people's ideas and knows how to build on them.	"Yes, and ..."
Imagineer	Is ready to think the unthinkable and explore the unknown.	"What if?"

24-HOUR CHALLENGE

Set yourself a simple challenge: in the next 24 hours, when you are in conversation with somebody, at some point force yourself to begin a statement with at least two of the word pairs above. It might be something as simple as "Why not meet up with Katy next week?" or "What if we were to invest in a new printer?"

You get bonus points if: (a) You manage to do this more than twice, and (b) any "Why Not?" or "What If?" statement you make is about what you might do rather than what the person you are talking to might do. (So "Why not just get out of the house and stop disturbing me" doesn't count!)

2
IDEA-BLOCKS AND MIND TRAPS

The ballpoint pen exercise in the previous chapter showed coming up with ideas is often a challenge. In some situations it's common for people to find themselves apparently unable to come up with any ideas at all, let alone ideas that are any good. More likely, those people (sometimes you?) are having ideas but dismissing them almost instantly because they are "silly", or impractical, or too risky, or just boring.

There are three types of block that are likely to be working against you even before you get as far as putting an idea into words. These are:

- A "Can't do" anxiety
- Your Inner Censor
- Your personal Mind Traps

We'll look at each of these in this chapter.

"CAN'T DO" ANXIETY

There are two common reasons that are given for not being able to come up with ideas:

"I DON'T HAVE IDEAS"

This is probably the most common creative block. It's common to dismiss your own ideas as unoriginal or impractical, to such an extent that you don't even think an idea ever happened. If you're in a job dominated by rules and procedures, where mistakes aren't tolerated, you may feel you simply aren't allowed to have ideas. It's certainly true that some people are more fluent at producing ideas than others. Sit in on a meeting with the scriptwriters of

The Simpsons or the creative team at an ad agency and most of us would feel feeble as idea-generators. Don't judge yourself against the creative geniuses.

"I DON'T HAVE THE TIME"

Is this a block, or is it just an excuse? If it's really important, you'll make the time. In any case, a lack of time isn't always a bad thing – sometimes it can actually help you to have ideas. Working to a tight deadline, you don't have time to think too hard about the drawbacks. That's one reason why improvised comedy is often funnier than scripted comedy that has been worked on for months.

YOUR INNER CENSOR

When you first have an idea, your brain will make judgements on the quality of the idea before you give it a chance to breath.

You may reject an idea because you think that it is:
* Impractical.
* Unoriginal.
* Boring.
* Dangerous.
* Ludicrous.

You don't want to share this idea with anyone else because (you predict) it will damage your reputation, and other people will question your judgement.

Here are two common thoughts that accompany new ideas:

"THIS WILL SOUND STUPID"

Most people feel anxious when they step out from the crowd. Putting forward an idea that is unusual or provocative draws attention to you. You might be laughed at or ridiculed, and the fear is also that people might look down on you for having dared to put forward such a poor-quality idea. That's why an idea is often defended by the person who suggests it when they start by saying: "I know this will sound stupid, but …" There are strategies for how to make it safe for you to put forward silly ideas in Chapter 6 (Giving Ideas).

"WHAT IF IT GOES WRONG?"

There are two reasons to be concerned about things going wrong. The first is that the mistake may be costly for you or others. If this is likely to be so, then of course you need to think through the consequences of your idea. But that shouldn't stop you having the idea in the first place. The second concern is that your reputation will be damaged. (I still recall my one effort at karaoke singing – it'll take a lot to persuade me to try that again!) One trait that marks out many creative thinkers is their ability to keep on trying, even if they suffer embarrassing failures along the way. I like the attitude of the inventor Buckminster Fuller who

> *"I haven't failed, I have just found 700 ways that won't work."*
>
> Thomas Edison (allegedly)

said: "There is no such thing as a failed experiment, only experiments with unexpected outcomes."

PERSONAL MIND TRAPS

Adults are often overly concerned about thinking and saying what they're expected to think rather than what they really think. Young children have a refreshing honesty about them, and divert their energy to new things that excite them. I've heard it said that there are three stages of life:

From **0 to 4 years** old is the **"Why not?"** stage.
From **5 to 11 years** old is the **"Why?"** stage.
From **12 onwards** is the **"Because"** stage.

The education system and the pressures of teenage life combine to make us into rational, conforming individuals who look for right answers rather than interesting ones. We become "Because" people.

So a lot of the time we kill ideas because we feel we are supposed to – or because we have been conditioned to follow rules and do things "the right way" as a part of being adult.

You don't have to spend long with young children to realize just how open they are to ideas and how geekily curious they can be (and there are ideas for how to tap into child-like curiosity on page 37).

Experience teaches us how not to make mistakes, but it can also trap us into making assumptions that prevent us from finding solutions. A puzzle helps to illustrate this nicely.

PUZZLE: JOINING THE DOTS

This Victorian puzzle has become synonymous with creative
thinking and the expression "thinking outside the box".
If you haven't seen it before, give it a go.
(If you have, see if you can still do it.)

Draw nine dots in a square, like this:

Your challenge now is to join all nine dots, using straight lines only,
and without your pen or pencil leaving the paper. You'll quickly find
a way of joining all the dots with five lines — for example, like this:

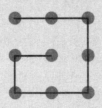

But can you find a way to do it using only FOUR strokes of the pen?

Finding a four-line solution is not easy – in fact, if this puzzle is new to you and you manage to come up with the four-line solution, then you're exceptional. (For the classic four-line solution, see page 144.)

Why do so few people succeed in finding the four-line answer? They get caught out because most people (including me when I first saw it) regard the square shape as a boundary and keep all the lines inside it.

It's quite a shock to think that we all tend to get trapped in this way, but we do so for a reason. To think outside the box seems inefficient, a waste of time or to some people even irrational. And yet it turns out that finding an approach that, in the short term, seems "irrational" proves to be the only way to come up with a perfectly rational solution.

However clichéd this puzzle may have become, I still think it's one of the best illustrations of the challenge of thinking creatively. We make assumptions all the time, creating our own artificial boxes, and it doesn't occur to us that we might need to go outside them. It turns out, however, that for the most logical of reasons, to think out of the box we sometimes have to allow ourselves periods of irrational play.

3
LATERAL
THINKING
(OR "WHAT'S
THE *REAL*
PROBLEM?")

One of the first steps to solving a problem creatively is deciding what problem it is that you are actually trying to tackle.

The term "lateral thinking" was invented by Edward de Bono in the 1960s and has entered our language. But what does it mean? Is it the same as creative thinking?

The word "lateral" suggests a sideways leap, and while you'll come across different definitions, I find it helpful to distinguish lateral thinking from creative thinking like this:

- **Creative thinking** is coming up with novel ideas for the problem you're presented with.
- **Lateral thinking** is addressing a completely different question from the problem you're presented with.

Sometimes it is lateral thinking that can give you the most radical and effective ideas of all.

This chapter shows you techniques for lateral thinking that can be particularly helpful if you feel trapped by a seemingly insoluble difficulty, sometimes by finding ideas that bypass the problem altogether.

THE LIFT PROBLEM THAT DISAPPEARED

According to office legend, there was once a company whose headquarters were in a tall building. Unfortunately, the lifts were extremely slow and staff began to complain about having to wait so long. Then the building manager came up with a brilliant solution. He installed mirrors outside the lifts, and the problem went away. Why? Instead of pacing around waiting, staff now spent their time using the mirrors to smarten up their appearance – tying ties, adjusting make-up and so on. Their complaints about the lifts stopped.

ANSWERING A DIFFERENT QUESTION

The story about the mirrors and lift in the box opposite is often quoted as an example of lateral thinking. The original problem – how to make the lifts go faster – was never solved. Instead, the building manager solved a different problem: how to keep people occupied while they wait.

Not everyone is happy with this bypassing approach, but the truth is that many problems we face in everyday life can't realistically be "solved" with the limited resources that we have.

The principle of answering a different question can be applied to just about any everyday problem. One of the most common problems for anybody responsible for a budget is: "How to reduce my costs this year." You may well have been a victim of bosses who tried to do this, often with cutbacks that ended up doing little apart from reduce morale. (I remember how, at one place I worked, the decision to replace the chocolate digestives with plain biscuits caused a disproportionate amount of ill will. Any saving on costs was probably far outweighed by reduced productivity.)

One of many ways of re-framing "How to reduce costs" is of course "How to increase revenue".

But how do you go about doing this re-framing? One approach can be to go back to child-like thinking.

KEEP ASKING WHY

Children love to ask "Why?" Often, they like this question so much they repeat it again and again. This can be a good way to wind up parents, but the "Why? Why?" technique has been a popular tool for problem-solving on factory floors for years. It works in more general everyday problem-solving too.

Imagine one morning your car won't start. The problem is clearly "I need to start the car" – the solutions to which are going to be things like "check the petrol", "read the manual" or even "call the roadside recovery people". But the "Why? Why?" approach might lead to a completely different sort of solution.

I need to start the car.
Why?
Because I need to get to work.
Why?
Because there's a meeting I need to get to.
Why?
Because I need to brief Colin on the plans for this week.

And so on. If the real problem is briefing Colin, maybe the solution is actually just to do a Skype call with him or defer the meeting until later, and – for the time being at least – nothing to do with starting the car.

Anyone who sits in meetings will be only too familiar with how easy it is to become bogged down in the detail of a problem. Here's one example that is typical of many. I was part of a committee organizing a conference for teachers. It had been decided that the conference should run as usual from Friday to Monday but some of us were worried that too few people would attend on the final day.

It probably took us half an hour of going into the minutiae of attendance figures, and thinking of ways to persuade people to turn up on Monday, before we found a solution. Instead of running from Friday to Monday, we would simply move the conference to run from Thursday to Sunday. Like many "out of the box" solutions, this one seemed obvious after the event. Yet when you're focusing on the details, such solutions can seem like a flash of inspiration.

The Monday solution could have been found in a couple of minutes if we'd simply applied the "Why? Why?" technique right at the start. Our thinking could then have gone something like this:

We need to find ways to boost attendance on the final day of the conference

Why?

Because most people we've spoken to won't be able to make it that day.

Why?

Because it's a Monday, when teachers will be wanting to prepare materials for the first week back at school.

Why does the conference have to finish on a Monday?

Because the conference is four days long and needs to include a weekend.

This process could have continued for several more stages, with each "because" generating ideas. In fact, the solution came from the third "Why?", "Why does the conference have to finish on a Monday?", to which the answer was: "It doesn't!"

AND ... WHO, WHAT, WHERE, WHEN AND HOW?

Asking "Why?" is a powerful way of opening a problem up. A second question, that can be equally helpful, is "Who is stopping you?" And you can dig even deeper into the problem with other simple questions: "What?", "Where?", "When?" and "How?" These all help you to bring relevant issues out into the open, and exploring every aspect of the issue can often suggest different points of entry.

The box opposite gives some examples of each type of question, showing how they can reveal particular aspects of a problem. As you can see in most of the examples, the main questions might easily lead on to associated questions, which can eventually point you in the direction of new ideas and possible solutions.

"I keep six honest serving-men
(They taught me all I knew);
Their names are What and Why and
When and How and Where and Who."

Rudyard Kipling

WHO	is part of the problem? ... Are there any other people I can involve?
WHAT	is the problem? What is it that is stopping me from acting? What objects or ideas could I do without? What else could I use?
WHERE	am I planning to solve the problem? ... Why not do it somewhere else?
WHEN	am I planning to address the problem? ... Why not do something about it sooner, or later?
HOW	am I going about tackling the problem? ... Is there another way?

EXPLAIN THE PROBLEM TO A CHILD

The "Why?" questioning above was inspired by the inquisitive approach that children have. You can tap into child-like thinking in other ways, too. If you are trying to find a new approach to a complex situation, think how you'd explain it to a young child. How would you explain it in a way that they'd understand? How could you turn the problem into a story?

CALLING IN THE "CONSULTANTS"

The Civil Service College used to run a two-week programme for high-flying managers – serious decision-makers who had been tipped as the next leaders. For several years I ran a creative-thinking workshop as part of the programme. My workshop always included an exercise where I would tell the delegates that they were about to meet some of the most creative consultants they'd ever encountered. These consultants, I would say, worked in an organization where they were encouraged to use their imagination every day. The consultants had a reputation for always wanting to explore and experiment, and had no qualms about offering their own radical ideas for solving the world's problems.

Then the "consultants" were invited into the room. They were eight-year-old children from the local primary school.

Each executive was then allocated three or four children, and challenged to explain to the children their job and a problem they were trying to solve. The children were asked to draw pictures and offer ideas for solving the problem.

The children's ideas were often naive and simplistic, but that's exactly what gave some of them so much impact. Sometimes it takes a child to point out what adults are unable or unwilling to see.

Most important of all, the jargon that often infests adult lives is useless with children. Having to return to plain, simple English helped to unclutter the managers' minds, and the real issues shone through.

Many senior managers found this exercise extremely tough, and a bit scary. But they never forgot it, and for some it proved to be one of the most effective ways of changing their mindsets.

PUZZLE: CAN YOU THINK LIKE A CHILD?

Here is a puzzle that I often pose to children. Try to put yourself
in the mind of a ten-year-old — can you think of the three
solutions that a class of children will usually come up with?
And can you find the solution that the Robinson family actually
adopted, which is the most elegant one of all?

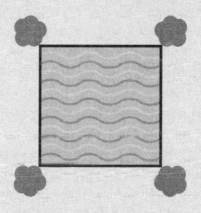

The Robinson family had a square swimming pool in their garden.
At the corners of the pool were four trees. The Robinsons wanted
their pool to be twice as big, and still square. However, they weren't
allowed to cut down the trees.

How could they make the pool twice as big and still square?

MAKING IT SIMPLE

If you don't know a child to ask for advice, try one of the following methods to help you to simplify a problem so you can reach its essence.

- Write down the problem in one short paragraph. Then reduce that paragraph to a sentence of no more than ten words. Now reduce it to three words. The ultimate challenge is to reduce the problem to one word.

- Explain the problem to somebody for whom it's completely unfamiliar. Then ask them to state the problem back to you. Their version is bound to be simpler. If they get it wrong, explain which part they've misinterpreted and ask them to state it again.

- Draw the problem as a diagram or picture (maybe as a PowerPoint slide), adding in no more than five words for labels. Pictures can convey complex ideas in a very concise way.

- Instead of focusing on the problem, imagine what the solution will be, and state that in no more than ten words. Once you've identified the solution you are looking for, it should be easier to define the problem clearly (see more on this on page 46).

"Simple can be harder than complex: you have to work hard to get your thinking clean to make it simple."

Steve Jobs

TURNING MOANS INTO "HOW TO" PROBLEMS

Even the most positive person likes to have the occasional moan: "Why can't I ever find a parking space?", "Why do we have to have so many commercials on television?", "Why does nobody ever tidy up their lunch dishes?"

There is an important difference between a moan and a problem. Moans are typically grumbles about things over which you have no control. They might feel therapeutic, but don't kid yourself that they'll improve your situation. Indeed, there are times when people indulge in moaning as a way of blaming somebody else when they have no intention of putting the situation right themselves.

A problem, on the other hand, is a situation that you can influence and want to change. However big or complicated it is, you should be able to find something you can do to make a difference.

One important step to being able to tackle situations

MOAN	PROBLEM
"Why can't they fix that noisy photocopier?"	"HOW TO (or How can I) find out who's responsible for the photocopier?"
"The traffic's always backed up at this intersection!"	"HOW TO find another way to get to my destination"
"The snacks we get here are lousy"	"HOW TO improve the snacks we get here" (or "HOW TO bring in my own snacks tomorrow")
"My wife/husband/partner doesn't understand me"	"HOW TO change my actions to get him/her to respond differently?"

creatively is to "re-frame", or change your view of, complaints by introducing the words "HOW TO".

You are turning your response from "Why don't they do something about it?" to "What can I do about it?" – which will make you more inclined to have ideas for how to solve the problem.

STARTING AT THE END

If you are tackling a complex, long-term problem, a more drastic way to re-frame it at the start is to imagine yourself in the future, when you have solved it. Once you've imagined your successful self, start to work backwards. Ask yourself how you got there. What was the final step? And the one before that? By tracking back all the way, you can create a plan for getting to your destination.

To bring this concept to life, you might imagine yourself in a particular situation, such as being interviewed by a journalist about your achievement. She might ask questions like the following:

- "What part of the project did you enjoy the most?"
- "How do you feel now that you've achieved your goal?"
- "How has your life got better?"
- "What was the biggest challenge that you faced? How did you get around it?"

This approach can help to give you new insights into what your real priorities are, and which problems are the most important to tackle.

PUZZLES: THREE LATERAL-THINKING QUICKIES

Question 1

If you check the statistics, you'll find that Canadians eat less in February than in any other month. Why is this?

Question 2

"How old are you?" Stan asked Sally. "A couple of days ago I was 12," Sally replied, "but next year I'll be 15." How can this be possible?

Question 3

The letters below are the start of a familiar sequence. Which letter comes next?

O T T F F S S

4
HAVING IDEAS
ON YOUR OWN

There are few things more satisfying than that moment of "Aha!" when an idea pops into your head. Being able to claim "it was my idea" can give you great kudos – as long as the idea goes on to be successful.

It's human nature to want to be associated with success, which is why, when a new invention takes off, there are often several people who lay claim to being the one who had the idea. (Meanwhile, strangely enough, it is often hard to find anybody who will admit to being the person who first had the idea if it resulted in a dud.)

The great thing about it being your idea is that if you have ownership of it you are more likely to want to see it through. It's important to remember this when it comes to sharing ideas with other people, because often if you want your idea to be implemented you might need to find ways to get other people to think it was (at least partly) their idea too (see Chapter 6, Giving Ideas).

There will be many occasions when you need to come up with ideas, and while having an "Aha!" moment is great, it is frustrating when ideas aren't coming.

So let's look at what you can do to help you to come up with ideas on your own.

RIGHT TIME, RIGHT PLACE

How is it that during the weekend your brain can be buzzing with ideas and projects and excitement, yet when it comes to Monday morning everything feels as if it's been switched off?

Your surroundings and your mood can have a huge

impact on your ability to have ideas.

Here are three things that are going to affect you:

- **The people around you** – if the people you are with don't tend to show any interest in you, or don't share your sense of humour, there is little incentive to start exploring ideas that you might need to discuss with them.
- **The place** – a bar full of people may make you feel buzzy, an art gallery reflective, while the boss's office might be intimidating.
- **The subject** – if it's something you're fascinated by or know plenty about, you'll have lots of ideas and opinions, but if you feel ignorant or uninspired, then the opposite will apply.

Can you influence these things? To some extent, yes.

- It's great if you can surround yourself with people who give you the confidence to express your ideas, but even if you can't do that, at least try to avoid having ideas around people who have a negative influence on you.
- Choose a place that makes you feel inspired. Several academic studies have revealed that being surrounded by greenery helps people to think more creatively. Even putting a pot plant on your desk has a positive effect.[2]
- If the subject doesn't fill you with enthusiasm, look for ways to make it more exciting (see silliness in Chapter 11).

---

2   Don't believe me? Read "Effects of an indoor plant on creative task performance and mood" by Shibata and Suzuki, 2004.

JUST DO IT!

Nothing can be more intimidating than a blank sheet of paper. Whether your challenge is thinking of writing a CV, preparing a big presentation or writing a novel, the opening few minutes … or hours … can be painful. Authors famously call it "writer's block". So how do you start?

Many artists, writers and composers will tell you the same thing. Just start somewhere. Anywhere. Which means you're allowed to start at the end if you want (which would mean preparing the final slide, or the final chapter, first.)

And don't be concerned about producing anything good in the first instance. The mere act of jotting down "any old trash" on a piece of paper can be enough to get the juices working. This is a one-person brainstorm, where you dump all your ideas without attempting to judge them on their quality.

Sometimes the only way to create something good is by producing something bad first. I once had a job on a team with a boss who was notoriously poor at briefing us when we wrote reports for him. We'd spend hours writing what we thought he wanted, only for him to cover our work with red ink and turn it into his own version. At first, we felt we were wasting our time, but then it dawned on us that our work acted as the catalyst for our boss's thinking.

The same principle can apply to your own work. An hour spent scribbling out a first draft that you finally throw away is not a waste of time. The mere act of getting these ideas down on paper lets you start to develop your thinking.

ORGANISING YOUR IDEAS

Ideas don't always come in a nice, logical order, they will often appear in a more haphazard fashion. If you put them down in a list, they may seem random and unconnected, and it can be helpful to find a way to note them down in a more organized way.

One of the best ways of dumping ideas on paper in a structured form is to use a spider diagram (it goes by many other names too – for example, Tony Buzan made famous a similar approach that he calls Mind Mapping).

In this technique, you start by putting the central problem or theme for your ideas in the middle of a page – this will be the "body" of the spider. As you think of sub-headings, you branch them off on a "leg" (and unlike real spiders, there's no rule for how many legs there should be). Each sub-heading will itself lead on to possible ideas, which can branch off on their own mini-legs (I suppose we should call them toes).

A simple example of a spider diagram is shown overleaf. This was a person who was trying to think of ideas for a thank-you gift for Aunt Maggie.

The advantage of this technique is that it draws your ideas out in multiple directions, rather than the single direction of a list. It also allows you to connect ideas by association, which mimics the way that the brain works.

It can sometimes almost feel as if the technique is drawing ideas out of you – if an area of the paper is blank, it begs to be filled by a new branch and new ideas.

Fans of this technique don't just use it as a method

of generating ideas. They also apply it for recalling information, taking notes or structuring a talk. You can use it in whichever way works for you.

"How can I know what I think until I see what I say?"

Graham Wallas, *The Art of Thought*

GETTING INSPIRATION FROM IDOLS

In the 1990s, evangelical Christians popularized the mantra "What would Jesus do?" and the idea of putting yourself in the mind of a role model has been used many times since. In the film *Finding Dory*, Nemo and his dad tackle problems by asking "What would Dory do?"

When looking for ideas to solve a problem, put yourself in the mind of a famous achiever or problem-solver and ask yourself how they would do it. For example, imagine we're looking for a way to stop people spraying graffiti on walls. If we allow ourselves a bit of simplistic stereotyping, here's how three famous names might approach the problem.

• John Lennon might, in his famous words, "Give peace a chance" and reason with the offenders – or he might make the walls into "Peace" walls, allowing graffiti with friendly, non-violent themes.

- Dorothy (from *The Wizard of Oz*) might get all emotional, using tears to pull on the heartstrings, make the offenders feel guilty and show them how their damage is affecting other people.
- Sherlock Holmes would look clinically at the evidence, detecting where graffiti artists were getting their materials and when they committed their offences, as well as discovering more subtle motives than those that the bumbling police worked out.

WARMING UP FOR HAVING IDEAS

Before they start a game, sportsmen get themselves ready with a warm-up to get their muscles loose. The same principle can be true for having ideas. When your brain is energized and buzzing, ideas will flow more easily.

- **Physical activity**
  Getting up and pacing around, or going for a walk or a jog, can click your brain into another gear. The activity gets your circulation going, making you more alert, and the change of scene will also stimulate your mind.
- **Stimulating music**
  Much has been made of the "Mozart effect", in which listening to Mozart is said to enhance your thinking skills. But the music doesn't have to be Mozart – depending on your taste in music you might experience the same effect by listening to a few minutes of Enya, Ella Fitzgerald or The Beatles.

- **Humour**
  Creative thinking and laughter are closely linked. One reason why we laugh is because we've heard something that doesn't fit our normal view of the world; in the same way, creative ideas are ones that overturn our expectations. If you're feeling bereft of ideas, find something or someone to make you laugh – watch a stand-up routine or a Bugs Bunny cartoon on YouTube.

However, you can take this even further by deliberately doing something apparently unconnected …

USEFUL DISTRACTIONS

I once asked a composer how he created a new piece of music. Did he take a blank sheet and wait for ideas? Not at all: he said that ideas only came when he was doing something completely different. This answer is typical of many creative professionals – and it could help you, too.

The best type of distraction is a mundane task that needs some concentration. For the composer, that might be sorting papers or research, but it could also be non-musical, such as doing the ironing, or a more fiddly activity such as doing a jigsaw puzzle.

"We often talk about the Three B's: the Bus, the Bath, and the Bed. That's where the great discoveries are made in our science."

A Scottish physicist, quoted by Wolfgang Köhler

The inventor Thomas Edison liked to go fishing. He had no intention of catching fish: he simply wanted time to himself.

But before you distract yourself, you should first immerse yourself in the task for which you are seeking ideas and solutions. For example, write down what you are trying to achieve or do some reading around the topic. Spend a bit of time actually trying to solve the problem even if you feel like you are getting nowhere. Then stop and move on to your distraction. Your subconscious will still be working on the problem, and diverting onto another activity will help it.

STORING IDEAS

Often it isn't enough to have a good idea: timing can be crucial as well. Too many good ideas are lost because they appeared at the wrong time and weren't even recorded. Yet your old ideas can be one of the best sources of inspiration.

Ideas can pop up in the most inconvenient places: while you're driving, or during a sleepless moment at four o'clock in the morning. They can flit away and be lost unless you record them.

These days anyone with a smartphone can record ideas as they crop up. (A pen and the back of an envelope work too, if you prefer old technology.) Get into the habit of noting down ideas that occur to you "at the wrong time". Keep them in an unused ideas file. Later on, when your mind is drawing a blank, you can then revisit these ideas for inspiration. It doesn't matter if they are bad ideas, because bad ideas can be a great stimulus for good ideas.

If you're a meticulous filer, you could categorize your unused ideas and keep them in separate folders. However, if you're a disorganized sort (like me) then just dump all your jottings into one file. The random jumbling of ideas can be exactly the jolt that your thinking needs at some future date. And this can lead on to ...

SERENDIPITY – AND HELPING ACCIDENTS TO HAPPEN

Sometimes defined as "a happy accident", serendipity is the discovery of valuable things that you weren't actually looking for. By definition, you can't make serendipity happen, but you can increase its likelihood by trying new things.

SYNTHETIC DYE – AN ACCIDENTAL INVENTION

Many of the world's greatest inventions were the result of accidents or mistakes. A classic example was the invention of a purple dye that is still popular today. It emerged, quite by chance, from the search for a cure for malaria.

For centuries, it had been known that quinine was an effective way to treat malaria. Unfortunately, natural supplies were limited, and by the 19th century chemists were keen to find a way to make quinine artificially. One such chemist was William Perkin. In one of his attempts, Perkin created a dark substance that dissolved in alcohol to form a purple liquid. He discovered that the liquid was an effective dye for fabric. Perkin had accidentally invented the first synthetic dye, which he called mauve.

One way to encourage serendipity is to set yourself a task that takes you out of your normal experience. In one example, the comedian Dave Gorman took on a bet to find 54 people across the world who shared his name. The task itself was pointless, but it led to rich experiences that turned into a TV programme, an off-Broadway show and a book.

ENCOURAGING SERENDIPITY

What pointless challenge can you set yourself to make serendipity possible? You could try one of these.

- Take a different route to work, or use another form of transport.
- Choose a different time of year to go on holiday.
- Buy an item from a store that you've never entered before.
- Look online or in your local newspaper or library at the list of public events going on next week. Pick the third one and go to it.
- Buy a magazine that you've never looked at before and read the editorial.
- Go to a section of a bookstore that you don't normally visit and choose a book with a title that catches your interest. Any book, from a novel to a "How to" book, might take your mind on a novel journey.
- Next time you plan to go out to the cinema, roll a dice to choose which film you will go to see.
- Become famous for five minutes. Phone up a local radio show to talk about a topic that interests you – or just enter one of their competitions.

PUZZLE: A SURPRISE IN THE MIRROR

How often have you looked in a mirror in your lifetime? Probably thousands of times. With all that experience you ought to have no problem with the following question.

Imagine you're standing close to a vertical mirror (such as a door on a bathroom cabinet), and can see down to your navel. You step back a few feet. Can you now see:

A more of yourself (that is, you can now see below your navel),

B the same amount or

C less of yourself?

5
EXCHANGING
IDEAS

Many (maybe most) situations where you are having ideas will involve a second person. You might be trying to solve a problem or come up with ideas with your partner, a work colleague or a family member. Ideas even come up when casually chatting with a friend on the phone.

When it comes to having ideas, involving a second person is generally a good thing. Two heads really can be better than one – the example of the accountant who suggested the answer XYAA in the puzzle on page 20 was a nice demonstration of how the second person doesn't have to be a particularly creative individual to be able to come up with ideas that will give you a second perspective. But involving a new person can also lead to problems.

This chapter has tips on how to make the most of a second person, and also how to avoid the common pitfalls.

SEEKING A SECOND OPINION

Even if you've had an idea on your own, the chances are that if you decide to take it further, a second person will become involved as a sounding board. Being able to talk through your ideas without someone interrupting or laughing at you can help you to form and refine them. Remarkably, a second person can still help you to develop ideas even when they don't say anything. Maybe you've had the experience of telling somebody about an idea, receiving only understanding nods in response, and at the end finding yourself saying, "Thanks. That really helped!"

It also helps to be questioned. There are bound to be things you haven't considered, and somebody who's unfamiliar with the problem you are trying to tackle will ask testing questions, so they can understand.

TWO SEPARATE ROLES: IDEA-GIVING AND IDEA-RECEIVING

Whenever you're discussing ideas with somebody else, you might find it helpful to think of it as a game in which you are dividing your time between two roles. Part of the time you'll be giving ideas to the other person; the rest of the time you'll be receiving their thoughts. You need to be able to play both roles well to have the best chance of generating ideas. (In the next two chapters we'll look at some of the tactics for how best to play these two roles in more detail.)

THE VICIOUS CIRCLE OF IDEA-KILLING

Unfortunately, when there are two of you involved there is also an increased risk of idea-killing. When you share an idea with somebody, you are inviting them to react to it. What you hope will happen is they will say "That's great, do it!"

What happens in reality, with most people most of the time, is that the idea gets questioned, challenged, laughed at or just rejected out of hand. That sounds brutal, but idea-killing comes as second nature to us, and it's so automatic we don't even notice it. Often we kill ideas just by ignoring them, and they quietly die on the spot. Just as often, people openly reject an idea by saying "Oh you couldn't do that because …" It's not usually meant to be negative, they are just trying to help. The message is: "Look, I can immediately see that idea isn't going to work, let me save you from wasting your time on it."

And once one idea has been killed in this way, what was meant to be an idea-generating discussion becomes an idea-killing argument.

The diagram below indicates how the vicious circle can begin. It can all happen so quickly, too. Becky gives an idea to Andy, who sees only the negative aspects, and so rejects it. Becky feels affronted by his response. To regain her status, Becky looks for faults in Andy's next idea. He, in turn, takes revenge, and the discussion descends into a conflict.

This vicious circle arises so often in conversations that you shouldn't have much difficulty spotting it, at home or in the workplace. This is how many family arguments start.

AVOIDING THE NEGATIVE CYCLE

It is possible to avoid getting into negative idea-killing cycles – but the person who is most in control of doing this is you. You need to remember one of the basic rules of creative discussions – generate an atmosphere in which people feel confident and supported, not "got at" and defensive.

The easy way to do this is to ensure that your first reaction to an idea from somebody else is always constructive. When the other person offers their idea, pick out the good points and build on them, using language such as, "That's a good idea, and what you could do is …", or "Yes, and that would help because …" ("Yes, and …" at the start of a sentence is one of the magic pairs of words to encourage creative thinking. It's hard to start a sentence "Yes, and" without it being creative, in the same way as it's hard to start with "Yes, but …" without it being an idea-killer.)

What's remarkable is that you can, with practice, develop the knack of turning a vicious circle of idea-killing into a virtuous circle of idea-building. The secret is simply to react positively to somebody's idea. They, in turn, will be more inclined to be positive about your ideas.

The diagram below shows how to generate a virtuous circle in which ideas flow freely. Note that the responses are positive from the outset. Becky gives an idea to Andy, who might not particularly like it, but still looks for positive points. He builds on those points by saying "Yes, and …" Becky feels encouraged by his reaction, and becomes more receptive to his ideas. She responds positively to Andy's next idea. Both are now in the right frame of mind to come up with new ideas.

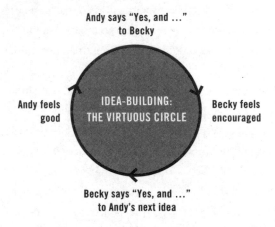

Andy says "Yes, and ..." to Becky

Andy feels good

IDEA-BUILDING: THE VIRTUOUS CIRCLE

Becky feels encouraged

Becky says "Yes, and ..." to Andy's next idea

LOOKING FOR A THIRD WAY

Often when two of you are exchanging ideas, it is because you are trying to negotiate a solution to something that you disagree on. The essence of successful negotiation is reaching a solution that everyone can accept. If you manage to do this by finding a compromise, all well and good. However, sometimes the middle ground doesn't fill anyone with enthusiasm. In that case, you need a new idea that will be equally appealing to everyone involved.

When foreign leaders get together to exchange ideas about saving the planet or preventing war, diplomacy is essential to their discussions. If you listen to a joint press conference held by two countries that are known to have major differences in policy, what will stand out is the effort that both countries' leaders or spokespeople make to emphasize the areas where they agree.

Finding common ground between people is just as relevant on an individual level as it is in international politics. It's a necessary goal, whether you're deciding with neighbours who should pay what to repair a shared fence or when debating with an ex-spouse where your children will go on holiday.

One way to generate new ideas in these circumstances is to begin by defining and agreeing on your objectives. What is it that both of you are trying to achieve? What issues are the most important for each of you? Once you have this framework for your discussion, you can think of ideas that will meet those objectives.

NOT BLACK, NOT WHITE, BUT YELLOW

There is, of course, a risk that you'll come up with a bland compromise that doesn't really satisfy anyone. If you think of one person's idea as "black" and the other's as "white", you could imagine the compromise idea as "grey". However, it might be possible to find a creative solution that excites both parties – you could think of this new idea as "yellow".

Black-and-white thinking is a particular hazard when emotions are involved. So, for example, a local community might find themselves in the sort of heated dispute outlined in the box below. You can reach the yellow state by using some of the lateral-thinking techniques described in Chapter 3 to help you decide what the real problem is and then bypass any areas where you're stuck.

THE DISPUTE OVER DERELICT LAND

In my local town, there was a dispute after a bit of disused land was taken over as a hangout for teenagers. The teenagers were leaving litter and the local residents reckoned if it wasn't nipped in the bud now, it wouldn't be long before there was drug-taking and discarded needles too. The dispute between teenage groups and the local community hit the local news headlines. The argument came down to this:

Teenagers' view ("white")

"This space is open, so anyone can just walk in here; we may as well hang out here ourselves."

Local community view ("black")

"These teenagers are noisy and that space is becoming dangerous."

Compromise ("grey")

"Fence off the space with a gate so that access can be restricted."

Real issue

This was a piece of wasteland that was of no use to the community in its current state.

Creative solution ("yellow")

In the end what the town did was invest in redeveloping the site to make it a community space, with an outdoor gym, table tennis, some flowerbeds and benches. Teenagers still used it, but so did families and the elderly.

MESSY CREATIVITY 1:
SYDNEY OPERA HOUSE

The Sydney Opera House, designed by the Danish architect Jørn Utzon, has become one of Australia's greatest icons, and the view of the Opera House with the Harbour Bridge as a backdrop is one of the most photogenic in the world. Yet its design and construction became, for a while, a source of ridicule and embarrassment.

The idea was simple and beautiful: to have a building reminiscent of a tall sailing ship passing through the harbour. The original design had interlocking roofs, much as we see today – but each roof had a complex curved shape, which made tiling them hugely difficult and expensive. It was only when somebody thought of shaping the roofs as segments of a sphere that the problem was solved.

Massive overspending, compromises and last-minute design changes all plagued the project. Yet when the Opera House was finished, 16 years after starting, the public forgave everything, and people around the world have loved it ever since.

6
GIVING IDEAS

Why might you give an idea to somebody else? You could be sounding them out to see what they think of your idea. Or you might be working jointly with them to come up with creative ideas, and this is your contribution. Or perhaps your idea is a suggestion for something you think they should do – you want to persuade them to take your idea on board, but find that they need to be convinced. Each of these situations counts as "idea-giving", but you'll need different tactics to ensure a creative outcome.

IF YOU'RE TESTING OUT AN IDEA ...

Let your colleague know what kind of response you're looking for. Sometimes, you might float ideas because you need support. If you've set your heart on resigning from your job to travel around the world, the last thing you'll want to hear is, "What, are you mad? This'll be a disaster for your career!" So, before you put forward the idea, set out what sort of response you are looking for by saying something like: "I need some reassurance – give me some reasons why I'm doing the right thing!"

On the other hand, you might be testing out an idea and looking for constructive criticism. If you know your idea is half-baked, warn your listener that it needs to be built on, and ask them to suggest ways in which you can improve it.

IF YOU ARE JOINTLY PRODUCING IDEAS ...

Set some ground rules at the start, to make sure ideas flow freely and you both stick to the point of the discussion. The simplest rule is that you'll have an initial period when you both put forward ideas without any evaluation. If this rule isn't set at the start, there's a danger that you will all too quickly criticize[3] and squash each other's ideas.

Each of you will tend to be more interested in your own[3] ideas than your partner's, but don't assume that your ideas will all be heard or recorded. If you have ideas that don't seem to have been taken up, make a note of them – you might be able to use them later.

IF YOU'RE "SELLING" IDEAS TO SOMEBODY ELSE ...

You may be convinced of the merits of your idea, but why should the other person "buy"? Imagine how you'd go about selling something to a sceptical purchaser. First, you need to draw their attention to the problem that your idea is helping to solve. Then, tell them the benefits of the idea, including the opportunities that it might open up. Finally, rather than presenting the idea as a finished article, let the other person adapt and build on it. People are generally much more receptive to ideas if they feel some ownership and if you let them participate in the creative process.

USE THE RIGHT WORDING

The wording that you use to present ideas can make all the difference between an idea being accepted and built on or being dismissed out of hand. If you tell somebody what they should do, you risk putting them on the defensive.

---

3   If you have, say, a whiteboard where you can jointly record ideas, this can really help.

However, if you offer ideas as suggestions, you leave space for the idea-receiver to adapt the idea and take some ownership of it.

There are some clear dos and don'ts for the language that you should use when offering ideas:

If you're dealing with somebody that you expect to be defensive when you offer ideas, think twice before starting with words like these:

- "What you (we) should do is …"
- "I think you ought to …"
- "The best idea would be to …"
- "If I were you I would …"

Instead, put forward your idea in "suggestion" form. Where possible, take out references to "you" and make the suggestion impersonal, as in the following examples:

- "I wonder if it would be possible to …"
- "Has anyone ever thought of …"
- "I don't suppose we could …"
- "What if it were …"

If you listen to conversations where a difficult situation is being discussed, you'll probably hear somebody saying: "I know this will sound stupid, but …" What the idea-giver is doing here is attacking themselves so that the idea-receiver doesn't have to. And more often than not, it works. Ideas of the type "I know this sounds stupid…" are often the most interesting ones, too.

HOW SUGGESTING BEATS PROPOSING

Psychologists have found that in general the more assertively you express an idea, the more likely it is that the person hearing it will resist it. In his book *Improve Your People Skills*, Peter Honey described an experiment in which people offered ideas in one of two ways:

- Proposing (when the idea is given as a statement, such as "What you should do is ...")

- Suggesting (when the idea is expressed as a question or a reflection: "I wonder if ...?")

The discussions were observed to see how the idea-receivers reacted to the ideas that they were given.

The results were remarkable. When an idea was proposed, almost half of the recipients received it sceptically and expressed difficulties with it.

Yet when the same idea was merely suggested, only one in five recipients stated difficulties. The more moderate way of putting forward an idea almost doubled the chance of the recipient supporting it, and halved the number of negatives.

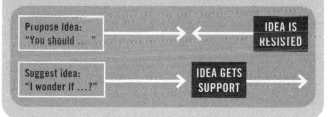

7
RECEIVING
IDEAS

We'd probably all prefer to think of ourselves as idea-givers (see Chapter 6) – after all, that sounds like the creative bit. Yet arguably the more important role is idea-receiving, because that is what sets the tone for building on ideas later.

If you want somebody else to help you generate ideas, then your responses to your friends' or colleagues' thoughts will have a huge bearing on whether they give you plenty of material to work with or dry up after only a couple of suggestions.

Here are some tips for being a creative idea-receiver:

SAY WHAT YOU NEED

Explain the problem clearly, and tell the other person which aspect you need their help with – otherwise, how can you expect them to come up with suitable ideas? This point may sound obvious, yet all too often you'll hear somebody asking for ideas and being met with silence because the other person doesn't know how to respond. Briefing your listener clearly will enable you to make the most of their contribution.

WELCOME ALL SUGGESTIONS

Don't set the standard of ideas too high. If you do, you may not get any suggestions at all, because the idea-giver will censor themselves. You can help by offering some rules, such as, "Please give me any idea, no matter how feeble you think it is." To make the idea-giver more comfortable, you can deliberately suggest a weak idea as an example. Your listener might then feel more confident that they can do better, and is more likely to offer a suggestion.

ALWAYS RESPOND

Whenever you receive an idea, you should acknowledge it and preferably give some constructive feedback. Otherwise, the idea-giver will assume that they've failed or you're not interested. To me this is the golden rule of idea-receiving, yet it's broken depressingly often.

PREMATURE EVALUATION

Next time somebody asks for your opinion about a new idea, try to observe what your immediate reaction is. Do you find yourself saying something like, "You couldn't do that because ...", or "Ah, what you don't know is ..."? Responses like these are natural, but they can kill the creative process stone dead

Why do we tend to react so negatively? In some cases, we have the best of intentions: we don't want the person to waste their time and energy. However, we might also do it for the following reasons:

- We're brought up to look for correct answers. Faced with an idea that isn't perfect, we feel obliged to point out its flaws.
- New ideas can be threatening. Their existence may make us feel that we're not doing our job properly, or that we need to change.
- There's also a bias against ideas that are "not invented here". Ideas often seem so much better when they're "ours".

Dennis Sherwood, an innovation guru, calls this tendency to react negatively to new ideas "premature evaluation".

Evaluation is important, but premature evaluation doesn't just snuff out someone else's creative spark: it can also prevent you from seeing new possibilities. Learn to pause whenever you hear a new idea, and take time to think about it and look for its good points first.

FINDING THREE POSITIVES

Rejecting a new idea is a normal reaction – even more so when the idea is about an issue close to your heart. Unfortunately, by doing so you send out signals that you're not receptive to change. Not only do you close off that avenue for exploration, but you also tread on the other person's ego.

Nobody enjoys having their ideas squashed, so this person is likely to react defensively, especially if they also feel strongly about the issue. You risk getting into the sort of "idea-killing" argument described on page 66. To stop this happening, you need to take a deep breath and be constructive.

There's an extremely effective tool that can take the negativity out of idea-receiving. If someone offers an idea to which you feel hostile, the rule is that you have to first build on it by deliberately looking for three good things that you can say about it, before you allow yourself to say anything negative.

"HERE ARE THREE GOOD THINGS ABOUT YOUR IDEA ..."

You'll probably find it's relatively easy to think of one positive thing about an idea that's been put to you, but it can be much more difficult to think of the second and third. A conversation in which three positives are given might go something like this:

- **Person A:** "What you should do is ..."
- **Person B (secretly biting tongue):** "What I like about that suggestion is:

   (1) it would ...

   and (2) it would ...

   and (3) another advantage would be ..."

This does put all the pressure on Person B. It takes broad shoulders to be constructive about an idea, especially if the idea is an implied criticism of what you've done.

And yet, if you force yourself to do it, the great advantage of this technique is that it takes a lot of the emotional sting out of the conversation. Not only that, but by the time you've had to think of three positive things about somebody else's idea, you can begin to see that there might even be a little bit of merit in it. Your colleague, meanwhile, having had some positive feedback, will be more receptive to your criticisms that follow.

And when it does (finally) come to you being negative about the idea, how should you phrase it? You could, of course, just let it all out with: "But overall, I think that idea is crap." But the more subtle way to offer the negatives is not by presenting them as "This idea is bad", but instead turning the criticism into a problem to solve: "How could we do this without it getting me sacked?"

AVOIDING A WEDDING CLASH

Here's an example of how a constructive idea exchange might go using an example of a wedding, which is a notoriously delicate area for idea-giving. The mother is the idea-giver, the daughter is the idea-receiver whose job it is to keep the conversation constructive.

Daughter: "We're just starting to come up with ideas for the wedding."

Mother: "I think you should hold it in the family church – it'll be the perfect place to bring all of your relations together."

Daughter (who has in mind a small humanist ritual somewhere out of town): "Well, what I like about that idea is:

1. I think churches are a good way of making it a spiritual event.
2. I do want to have close family members there.
3. It's important that the venue has some meaning for us."

Only now does she express her reservations: "However, Peter and I don't want a traditional religious service, and we'd prefer to have the wedding in a place that has spiritual significance for both of us. What sort of venue would work for that?"

At this point, the family church idea might be rejected, but at least the daughter has now helped to clarify what she's looking for. By thinking through some of the benefits of her mother's idea, she might find some elements that she could take on board. In addition, the even-handed nature of the discussion might make her mother feel more positive about the eventual result, because her feelings have been taken into consideration. Nobody says this sort of exchange is easy, but at the very least it would be good if a family argument can be avoided.

24-HOUR CHALLENGE

Do you dare to have a go at this? Sometime in the next 24 hours, somebody will probably suggest an idea to you. Try to remember not to react to it in the normal way; instead, see if you can give them three reasons why you like it (and don't reveal that you are using a technique you just read in a book). It may not be comfortable, but the outcome might be interesting.

SUGGESTION SCHEMES

In the workplace, a common method of getting ideas from others is through suggestion schemes. You may also see requests for suggestions anywhere from restaurants to railway stations. Unfortunately, suggestion schemes are rarely successful, and the main reason for this is that the people putting ideas forward don't expect to get any feedback and assume their ideas are going to be ignored, or even worse, criticized.

I saw an example of a successful suggestion scheme at the BBC's recording studios, in the days before e-mail. In each studio was a book where users could comment on the equipment and suggest any improvements. The book was brimming with comments. The reason why there were so many suggestions was partly down to a rule for giving feedback: every idea had to get a handwritten, constructive response within 24 hours, even if it was simply, "Thank you, this is a complicated issue. We're looking into it." People felt that their comments mattered, so they continued to make suggestions.

If you can't respond to every idea, at least let people know how much feedback you can handle. A company I once worked with had what they called the "Unsolicited Ideas Box". This box was there for every employee to use. It came with a promise that every idea put in the box would be read by the CEO, and the person making the suggestion could remain anonymous. However, there was no guarantee of any feedback. For people who wanted feedback, there was a more formal suggestion scheme. Interestingly, the Unsolicited Ideas Box proved to be more popular than the formal scheme.

"To profit from good advice requires more wisdom than to give it."

Wilson Mizner, playwright

MESSY CREATIVITY 2:
THE DISCOVERY OF DRUGS

The history of drug development is riddled with accidental discoveries and neglect. The most famous example is penicillin. The Scottish biologist Alexander Fleming returned to his lab one morning to discover that some dirt had blown through the window and killed the bacteria he was cultivating.

The invading substance was a mould called *Penicillium notatum*. What is less well known is that this accident happened in 1928 – more than 13 years before the first successful treatment of a human patient. The discovery lay dormant because Fleming didn't regard it as having much practical use. It took hard work, ingenious insights, and trial and error by other scientists in England and America before penicillin could be produced in significant quantities for medical use.

Nitrous oxide, one of the first anaesthetics, has a similar history. The gas was discovered in 1795, but was used just for entertainment, as a laughing gas, for the next 50 years. One night, at a laughing-gas demonstration, a volunteer who tried it was found to have gashed his leg and not felt anything. By chance, the man who noticed this effect was a dentist, who immediately thought of a good application.

8
HOLDING
IDEAS
MEETINGS

When there are more than two people involved in discussing ideas, the dynamics change completely. What we now have is a meeting. (Conversations between two people are also sometimes called meetings, but in this chapter meetings will always refer to three or more people discussing ideas together.)

Meetings to discuss ideas can be light-hearted and casual (three of you getting together in the pub, for example), but most meetings are quite formal and serious affairs. The most common place for meetings is the workplace but you'll also have meetings if you're on a committee of some kind, or if you're in a team that's planning a project.

In all but the most basic of information exchanges, a meeting will involve an exchange of ideas.

THE IDEA-KILLING MEETING

Imagine for a second that you are due to hold a meeting, but you have decided, for some conniving reason, that you want this meeting to produce no useful ideas whatsoever. It is in your power to decide who will attend this meeting, where it will take place and how it will run.

How would you run the ultimate idea-killing meeting? Perhaps you would use some of these tactics:

- **Invite a lot of people.** The more people there are in the meeting, the less air time each individual will get. Even with five people in a meeting, because only one person can talk at a time, each individual is only getting on average 20 per cent of the time in which they can speak. Holding a large meeting has another idea-killing benefit, too. It means that when you put forward an idea, you have a large audience – and most people find that intimidating.

- **Invite senior experts with reputations to preserve.** Experts are almost by definition idea-killers (see page 93). And, of course, the non-experts in the meeting will feel awkward knowing that their ideas are likely to come across as naive, so they will prefer to say nothing.
- **Every time an idea is raised, ensure that there's a chance for it to be pulled apart.** This should take the momentum out of any idea that has promise, and the number of ideas put forward will soon decline to a trickle.
- **Don't have any structure to the discussion.** It helps if the person "in charge" of the meeting is emotionally involved in the problem being discussed. That ensures they will focus on the detail rather than worrying about the process of the meeting, meaning you can veer off topic and get bogged down by unnecessary detail at every opportunity.
- **Don't have a formal way of recording the ideas that come up.** An idea that isn't recorded is quickly forgotten, except by the person who had the idea, who will then have only one thing on their mind, which is repeating the idea until (s)he is happy that it has been recorded.

If that sounds like the sort of meetings you usually attend, it might explain why they tend to be so unproductive when it comes to ideas.

It's one of the ironies of creativity that the most effective creative meetings have rules and a structure.

RULES FOR CREATIVE MEETINGS

Creative meetings need rules. Why? Because otherwise they will almost always turn into idea-killing meetings.

In a casual meeting, the rules can be low-key, and a very brief part of the start of the meeting: "Can we just start with everybody chipping in one idea, with no comments on the ideas from anyone else until we have been around the table."

In more formal meetings, where there are one or two dominating characters present, there can be rules that help to control the louder individuals and encourage the quieter ones; for example, by putting a limit on how many ideas the louder individuals are allowed to put forward.

One nice ice-breaking rule I came across involved everyone at the meeting being given three sweets at the start. Every time they wanted to put forward an idea they had to submit a sweet, and when they ran out of sweets they had to stay quiet for the rest of that section of the meeting. It immediately set a playful tone for the meeting, while also providing a clear, visible rule about participation.

APPOINT A REFEREE

Rules are quickly ignored if they don't get enforced from the start. Meetings usually have somebody called the "chair", but it can be more helpful to think of the person in charge of the meeting as being a referee (like a football referee). The referee need not be the most senior person present, but it does need to be somebody who is confident and who is trusted by the group. It's the referee's job to state the rules at the start of the meeting, and to be sure that they are applied firmly but fairly to everyone involved.

Sometimes when facilitating creative meetings I've reinforced this notion of the referee by having a yellow card with me. As soon as somebody breaks a rule,[4] such as pulling apart an idea in a session that's supposed to be free-flowing, I raise the yellow card with the warning that a second offence will mean a red card. It's all done in good humour, of course, but one warning is almost always enough. Even better, the group will usually begin to referee itself.

EXPERTS AS IDEA-KILLERS

The world needs experts. Where would we be without scientists who can interpret DNA, or lawyers who can get their heads around tax fraud? And the natural home of the expert is often meetings, the place where they can demonstrate their expertise in front of others.

Unfortunately, being an expert can be a huge barrier to you coming up with ideas.

I have a slightly cynical definition of an expert: somebody who knows every reason why a new idea won't work. It was experts who made the following disastrous pronouncements:

---

4   In my experience a rule usually gets broken in the first couple of minutes of an ideas meeting.

"Who the hell wants to hear actors talk?"

H.M. Warner, 1927.

"Guitar groups are on their way out."

Decca Recording Co. turning down The Beatles, 1962.

Do you ever go into "expert mode" when you're talking about wine, gardening or something else that you're particularly knowledgeable about?

How do you demonstrate your knowledge to other people?

Much of the time, you probably do it by responding to their ideas with comments like "That wouldn't work because ..." or "They tried that back in 2003 ..." While it may boost your ego to demonstrate expertise like this, it's also a surefire way of killing off other people's ideas.

Experts are important, particularly if you are looking to develop practical ideas that have a chance of being implemented. But in meetings, experts need to be managed, particularly on when and how they are allowed to give feedback on ideas that are put forward.

BRINGING IN AN OUTSIDER

Sometimes an outsider is able to offer suggestions that somebody within the group would never be allowed to make. The outsider will be somebody unfamiliar with your particular problem or the way things are done in your group, and therefore has "permission" to be naive and un-expert.

> *"For every expert there is an equal and opposite expert."*
>
> Arthur C. Clarke

If no outsider is available, you can even create one: "What would Richard Branson have said about this?" It can be easier to put across an uncomfortable idea if it's not "you" saying it. When my children were young, I often had greater success suggesting an idea if it came from Bertie the hand puppet than if I said it myself. If I told them to eat up the cabbage, they'd just resist. But if Bertie suggested it, they would often comply, or at least argue a reasonable case for not doing so. You might want to think twice before using a hand puppet with an adult, but anything that can help you put forward an uncomfortable idea through the mouth of somebody else is likely to make the exchange of ideas that much easier.

RECORDING IDEAS

It's common in the workplace to have a flipchart or even an interactive whiteboard in meeting rooms, as a place to record ideas. Yet in most meetings these aren't used. Why not? Mainly because of habit, and because it still feels a bit forced (or even a bit school-like?) to have somebody standing up recording ideas. This is understandable, yet if you can overcome the discomfort of using one of these devices, they can really help the creative process. One of the advantages of flipcharts and the like is that when ideas are noted down, everyone can see them. It gives confirmation that your idea has been correctly recorded (so you can move on to another idea). Having ideas on display also gives the group something to refer back to later in the meeting: "I liked Harry's idea, the second one down, when he said ..."

If having a board to record ideas on isn't possible in the idea meeting that you're having, the next-best option is to have an appointed note-taker. If they are doing their job – to record all ideas that come up in the meeting – they won't have much time to spend on anything else, such as having ideas themselves. And you do need to trust their judgement. Note-takers are often guilty of acting as an idea-censor, and only noting down the ideas that they like.

The ultimate way of recording ideas in a meeting is to film it. That's good if you want to be sure that every idea is captured, but not everyone is comfortable being filmed, and to capture the ideas some poor person is going to have to watch the entire meeting again later.

GETTING IDEAS FROM LARGE GROUPS

I regard a meeting of more than five or six people as being a large group. When a meeting is large it becomes even more scary to contribute an idea. If you're the person running a group discussion, try these tips to ensure you get as much contribution as you can from everyone present.

BREAK THE ICE

Open the discussion with an ice-breaker, to make people relax. For example, you could ask each person an easy, open question, such as, "What was the most fun thing you did last week?" Or you could encourage people to engage with the topic of discussion by asking, "What would you most like to come out of this discussion?" Another great ice-breaker, especially in "serious" meetings, is to crack open a packet of chocolate biscuits at the start. But if you do this, you must also make a show of eating the first one. There's nothing more stifling to the mood than being in a meeting with chocolate biscuits where nobody takes one.

SET THE BAR REALLY LOW

To get the ball rolling with ideas, start by suggesting a really bad idea and admit to the group that it's lousy. By doing so, you're giving the message that it's all right to offer any idea, however stupid it may seem. As a result, others will feel more confident about putting forward their suggestions.

BREAK UP INTO PAIRS

Break the large group into smaller groups, or even pairs. This helps you to avoid "Groupthink", and it also allows the participants to think at their own pace. Five pairs will have far more ideas in one minute than one group of ten people. In addition, everyone finds it easier to suggest ideas to one person rather than nine, and the fact that there are other groups thinking about the same issues can bring out a little competitive edge to spur people on.

ALLOW ANONYMOUS CONTRIBUTIONS

Never assume that because somebody says nothing it's

because they have nothing to say. Not everyone wants to be noticed or wishes to have their name linked to an idea, especially if it's a controversial one. So allow a time for anonymous contributions. Rather than making people say their ideas out loud, you can ask everyone to write them on slips of paper, and collect them in a bucket, or even give people Post-it® note pads and get them to stick their ideas on a wall. This can be an extremely effective way of getting a lot of ideas very quickly.

PUZZLE:
THE DICTIONARY BOOKMARKS

An illustrated dictionary comes in two volumes, and is sitting on the shelf. A–M is on the left and N–Z is on the right, as you would expect. Each volume is about 5cm thick, with covers that are about 3mm thick.

Somebody has bookmarked the entry for Aardvark in Volume 1 and the entry for Zebra in Volume 2, and the bookmarks are sticking out of the top of the books. How far apart are the two bookmarks (to the nearest centimetre)? There is no trick here but the answer might surprise you.

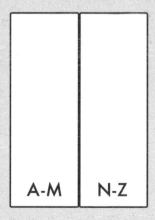

9
DEFINING
THE PROBLEM
IN MEETINGS

Chapter 3 looked at ways to figure out what problem you actually want to work on, and showed that stepping back to agree on what the problem is that you want to solve can lead to lateral thinking (that is, solving a different problem from the one you started with).

Taking time to understand the problem can be an extremely effective way to start a creative problem-solving meeting.

Any meeting is more effective if it has some sort of agenda, but when it's a meeting that is about finding solutions to a complex problem, a clear structure becomes even more important.

Without a structure, and a person in charge to manage it, a problem-solving meeting will rapidly fall apart, as the participants become muddled about what they're supposed to be doing. Without structure, a meeting will typically start with one person jumping in with an idea, another will dismiss it, then there'll be a heated debate, and it might be 20 minutes into the meeting before somebody pipes up with, "What are we actually trying to solve here?"

THE P-I-E OF PROBLEM-SOLVING MEETINGS

There is a simple structure that you can use in any problem-solving or creative-thinking meeting. It works on the P–I–E principle, as shown opposite.

This structure has three stages: by keeping the stages separate, you focus people's minds on particular tasks and ensure that everyone's energy is devoted to coming up with ideas, rather than worrying about what their role is.

P is for Problem

Start by agreeing what it is you actually want ideas for, and set the rules for the meeting at the same time. Otherwise, you'll find everyone will come up with their own, different view of what they're supposed to be doing.

I is for Ideas

Once you've agreed what you want ideas for, you should then have the "brainstorming" phase – all ideas welcome, no criticism allowed. (There's more about this in Chapter 10.)

E is for Evaluation

This is the stage when you're allowed to criticize ideas (constructively), and pick out the ones that have the most potential. (See Chapter 12.)

STATING WHAT THE PROBLEM IS

A simple, no-nonsense way to start a problem-solving meeting is just to go around all the participants asking them to state – in one sentence – what they believe is the nub of the problem to be tackled.

Let's suppose the issue of concern to a group is about improving internal communications (a problem that seems to crop up with most working groups). One person might describe the problem as: "How to be clearer about what everyone else is doing on the project", while somebody else might feel there is a more specific issue – for example, "How can we ensure everybody reads the weekly email update?" Each person's definition of the problem should be recorded (preferably on a flipchart) and then the group can decide, maybe by voting, which of the versions of the problem they want to work on first.

This process isn't very creative, but if the group is clear about what problem is being worked on, the process of having ideas to solve the problem is much more focused.

DAYDREAMING AND WISHING

Perhaps you would like your meetings to be more insightful, more creative and more engaging too? If so, there is a more adventurous technique you can use for defining the problem at the start, which is more likely to lead some lateral thinking.

First, let's be honest about meetings. Especially serious work meetings. When you are in a group meeting in the office and somebody is talking about "improving customer targeting" or "reducing outages on the production line", are you hanging on their every word, assessing the situation and coming up with a solution that meets all the constraints?

Maybe you are.

But more likely, you are only half-listening. Because really you are drifting in and out as you listen to the far-more-interesting meeting that is going on in your own head: "I wish Brian would just sack the current sales team …", you think; or, "Why can't we stop producing widgets, they don't make any money anyway", and even, "I wish I hadn't skipped breakfast, I could really do with lunch right now."

Instead of fighting this instinct to daydream, you can tap into it. While the logical part of the brain takes in facts and deciphers the language, the intuitive part goes off at a tangent, asking questions and making connections. Both processes are necessary, but the daydreaming side can be surprisingly helpful in defining what the problem really is.

You can exploit daydreaming in a very practical way using the "I wish ..." technique described below.

THE "I WISH ..." TECHNIQUE

When I worked with civil servants, they would often be dealing with complex administrative problems that they were trying to solve. I would often use the "I wish ..." technique with them. The person having to deal with the problem (the "problem-owner") would have the job of describing the problem as they saw it. They would

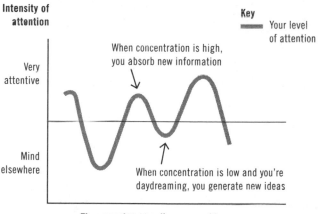

explain the background to the problem, why it needed to be solved and what they had tried so far. But (I made it clear) the problem-owner's real job was to keep talking, to be the droning voice in the background. Meanwhile, everyone else in the meeting had the role of being an idea-generator. They had to switch off their analytical brain, and allow themselves to just write down whatever half-baked thoughts they had on what the real problem might be.

They had a choice of how to write down problems. They could either write them in the form:

"How to …" (for example, "How to recruit more staff to deal with this problem").

Or they could write them as wishes:

"I wish …" (for example, "I wish you could just sack the lazy ones"). The words "I wish" are shorthand for: "I know this is silly, but here's a completely off-the-wall thought that occurred to me."

After a couple of minutes of rambling waffle (oops, I mean detailed description of the problem and its background) by the problem-owner, we'd collect 10 or 20 How-tos and I-wishes from the group who'd been half-listening. The problem-owner would then be able to choose from the list two or three that he felt were the real issue that he wanted help resolving.

Two things always struck me when we did this exercise.

The first was that even though the group had supposedly been "daydreaming", when it came to gathering in their How-tos and I-wishes the problem-owner always said that it felt as if the group had been listening *really well*.

The second thing was that the problem-owner almost *always* picked at least one "I wish …" as a problem he or she wanted to focus on. Far from being "silly", these ideas were often the ones that provided the lateral insight that was needed.

10
BRAINSTORMING
IN MEETINGS

People use the word "brainstorming" for any meeting in which people generate ideas. However, true brainstorming follows four main rules that were created in the 1930s by advertising executive Alex Osborn:

NO CRITICISM

During the idea-generating period, all ideas must be recorded. No negative comments are allowed and no idea should be rejected.

QUANTITY, NOT QUALITY

You should aim for 100 feeble ideas rather than 10 good ones. The thinking behind this is that, as Osborn said, "It's easier to tone down a wild idea than to think up a new one."

FREEWHEEL

Once the process has begun, you should allow the discussion to go where it wants to go.

BUILD

A successful brainstorm is one in which people pick up others' ideas and build on them. If you hear an idea and you respond by saying "Yes and …", then that means you're building.

These principles have always come naturally to those in the comedy business. The artists in the *Looney Tunes'* cartoon studios in the 1940s would spend hours developing ideas

in meetings at which negative comments were banned.
Bugs Bunny, Porky Pig and Road Runner were nurtured
using deliberate sessions of positive thinking.

HOW LONG SHOULD A BRAINSTORMING MEETING LAST?

I've known groups spend a day or more holding intensive
brainstorming meetings, but there needs to be a really
good pay-off if you're going to spend that much time
having ideas. The good news is that brainstorming meetings
can be very short and still be extremely productive; and,
of course, if a brainstorming meeting is really short, it
can hardly be branded a waste of time. I reckon that most
workplaces would be more productive and enjoyable places
to be if every work team had to spend five minutes every
week doing pure brainstorming. That's a trivial amount
of time in the grand scheme of things, but it's five minutes
more than most groups spend at the moment.

The worst that can happen is that those five minutes
produce nothing, but even if a brainstorming meeting
produces nothing of obvious value, it can still energize a
group. And a bit of fun is good for its own sake. There are
several enlightened companies, such as Innocent, producer
of the popular smoothies, who have built weekly game-
playing sessions into their culture because of the benefits
these have for team-building and fostering loyalty.

SETTING A TARGET

Sometimes all that's needed to generate ideas is a target. There's an exercise that I've conducted many times in workshops, in which the participants discover how to brainstorm effectively without needing to be given rules in advance. I tell the group that their challenge is to come up with new ideas for an Indian restaurant. They are to record their ideas on a flipchart.

If there are, say, eight in a workshop, I split them into two groups of four. I then hand the two groups a written briefing.

Group A are given the instruction: "*You have ten minutes to come up with NEW ideas for an Indian restaurant.*"

Meanwhile **Group B** are given this: "*You have ten minutes to come up with 50 IDEAS for an Indian restaurant.*"

Neither group knows that the other group's instructions are slightly different.

At the end of the exercise I ask both groups to count how many ideas they came up with, and to pick out their best two ideas.

The results are consistent and remarkable. Group A, which hadn't been given a target, typically report back that they had five or six ideas. Then, to the amazement of Group A, Group B announce they have come up with more than 50 ideas (they almost always beat their target). What is more, the "best ideas" put forward by Group B are invariably better and more exciting than those from Group A (they come up with Bollywood-themed ideas, Indian restaurants in supermarkets, curries presented as pizzas, and so on). Both groups were working on the same problem, but by giving Group B a ridiculously high target, they have no chance to evaluate the ideas they come up with and they end up working to the rules of brainstorming without needing to be told them.

HAVING A PLAN B

When you're caught up in an idea, you might not think to look for other avenues. Having one big idea is exciting, but a few minutes considering a "Plan B" will be time well spent. As the mathematician James Yorke said: "The most successful people are those who are good at Plan B."

Coming up with a Plan B is never easy. When a group gets stuck into an idea, and is getting carried along by the momentum, it's difficult to let go. This is fine if the idea works, but, more often, when you reflect on a concept later, you begin to see its flaws and it doesn't seem so great after all. The Plan B approach not only gives you a fallback option, it can often improve the quality of your main idea.

A USEFUL CATALYST

I once worked with a team that had been asked to come up with ideas for promoting a new exhibition at London's Science Museum. They became hooked on a concept that would involve staff dressing up as atoms and walking around the city linked together as a "molecule". It was suggested that they spend a few moments on a Plan B. There was some resistance, because they were enjoying themselves with the first idea. However, within ten minutes, they had produced an idea for advertising on trains, which they started to prefer to the first notion. In the end, they combined the two: the carriages became the atoms that were linked to make the molecule.

NEGATIVE BRAINSTORMING

Some of the most heartfelt opinions can be expressed only as comedy. That was one of the roles of the court jester in medieval times: the low-status fool was able to utter truths that would never be tolerated in those of high rank. And it applies in meetings, too.

People who are too shy to give their ideas formally often find it easier to speak up in a light-hearted setting. One of the easiest ways to make a dull or sensitive problem more "fun" is with negative brainstorming. The idea is simple. Instead of brainstorming "How can we improve X?" the group brainstorms the complete opposite: "How can we make X as bad as possible?"

Playing this game of opposites can work particularly well in any group where you want to get ideas out of people on a sensitive issue where they don't want to appear disloyal (especially in the workplace).

For example, it's common for junior staff in an office to complain about the need for "better communications". Instead of asking, "How could we make communications better?", to which the response is likely to be dark looks and silence, you can spend five minutes on the opposite: "How could we make communications here as bad as possible?"

This invariably generates laughter, particularly if it's teams where there are serious communication problems, and the permission for a bit of subversion allows people to state real concerns in a safe way.

MESSY CREATIVITY 3:
"YESTERDAY" AND OTHER SONG LYRICS

Once a song has entered the pop charts, its words become part of our culture, never to be changed. It's easy to forget that songs are like any other creative work, and go through numerous changes and revisions before they're set in their final form.

Most songs start as a fragment of an idea. Paul McCartney has told how he woke up with the tune for the song "Yesterday" in his head. In the absence of any lyrics, he decided to call it "Scrambled eggs" — words that fit the rhythm, but certainly don't have the sound of a smash hit about them.

Tim Rice has documented how the lyrics for *Evita*, the concept album that became a world-famous musical, went through countless redrafts as the deadline for producing the album approached. Do you recognize the song whose opening line, in one early draft, was: "All through my reckless and wild days," and in another was "It's only your lover returning"? Both of these lines were scrapped at the last minute, in favour of the line "Don't cry for me, Argentina".

11
INJECTING MORE SILLINESS

In Chapters 3 to 10 you've seen techniques for helping ideas to flourish, either on your own or when with other people.

Stepping back to see what the real problem is; using the right language when putting forward ideas; looking for the positive features in any idea; and having structured meetings in which there are clear rules – all of these things can improve creativity.

What's more, you could probably imagine using most of those approaches in everyday life, even among more cynical colleagues, without anyone thinking you were doing anything particularly unusual. Nobody will get punished for suggesting using a flipchart, or asking "Why?" a few times.

But sometimes, if you want really *new* ideas, you need to embrace more silliness. You need to come up with, and then see the potential in, ideas that are outrageous, dangerous, embarrassing, childish and downright stupid.

In doing this, you will not be alone. Some of the most creative professionals are people who work in the advertising industry. When you see some of their output, you might wonder where they got these ideas from. The answer is that you are only seeing the tip of the iceberg, the ads that make it to television are only the ideas that they allowed you to see. You don't get to see the scores of silly ideas that came up behind closed doors.

If you (or more importantly their client) could see some of the outrageous ideas they came up with, the ad agency would probably be fired on the spot. But the whole point is that most of those ideas did stay behind closed doors.

OPPOSITES

One of the handiest "silly" techniques is one we've encountered already. The technique of tackling the opposite problem was discussed on page 114, particularly as a way to inject humour and freshness into a stale problem.

"Opposites" is such a powerful technique, it can be used on just about any problem. It can be particularly helpful when you want to develop a new product or service, forcing you to think about a familiar concept in a completely different way.

At first sight, this technique seems absurd, but looking at the opposite of the problem can give surprising insights and perfectly sensible solutions.

For example, how do you get cars to go faster on a congested road? It turns out that one of the most effective solutions is to make them go slower.

This idea sounds like a riddle from *Alice in Wonderland*,

THE EXPANDED TROLLEY

The reversal technique was used to good effect by a designer I met who was trying to create a smaller catering trolley for use on an aircraft (so people could squeeze past in the aisles). In search of inspiration, he considered the reverse problem: how to make the trolley larger. His solution for a larger trolley was to run it on rails above the corridor (the only place where it would fit). If the trolley were larger, he could fit ovens inside to heat the food, and in turn the kitchen at the rear of the plane could be smaller so they could squeeze more seats into the plane. This idea turned out to be feasible and was subsequently patented. I'm waiting for the day when we first see an overhead trolley so I can say, "I remember the guy who came up with that idea."

but the explanation is quite logical. When cars are going fast, drivers have less reaction time and are prone to sudden braking, which can bring the traffic to a standstill. If cars are given a speed restriction of, say, 40mph, traffic moves more steadily and, like the tortoise versus the hare in Aesop's fable, people can arrive sooner at their destination. In the 1990s, the M25 motorway around London started adopting slower speed limits like this in order to speed up traffic. It was very successful, and many other motorways have adopted it since then.

CHALLENGE: TRY THE OPPOSITES TECHNIQUE

The opposites technique is the equivalent of the reverse gear in a car: it's a tool to use when you've reached a dead end. Have a go at using it with one of these three problems.

1 Remembering to send out Christmas cards in time each year.

2 Getting your children ready so you can take them to school.

3 Encouraging health and safety in the workplace.

What ideas do you come up with? There are some suggestions on page 147 at the back of the book.

TAKING THINGS TO THE LIMIT

You can also open up new avenues for problem-solving by taking the problem to the extreme. Instead of "How can we do this by tomorrow?", what if we changed the problem to "What if we had to do this in the next minute?" Or "Instead of needing to make an extra £100, what if

I needed to make an extra £1,000,000?" Exaggerating in this outrageous way blows the constraints of the problem out of the water, for a while at least, and allows your imagination to run riot.

For a problem you're currently faced with, for which you need ideas, try asking these questions – some will feel completely inappropriate to your problem, but give them a go anyway – and see where they take you:

• What if you did things in a different order?
• What if money were no object?

PRODUCTS THAT COULD HAVE BEEN THE RESULT OF AN "OPPOSITE" BRAINSTORMING:

ORIGINAL	OPPOSITE	RESULTING PRODUCT/SERVICE
You drive to the store to buy groceries	The store drives to you	Ocado and other home delivery
A handful of TV channels watched by millions of people	Millions of TV channels watched by a handful of people	YouTube
I drive the car	The car drives me	Google's self-driving car
Recording company decides which pop stars to promote to the public	The public decides which pop stars to be promoted by the recording company	*Pop Idol*, which led to *X Factor* and other audience-voting talent shows
Send electronic messages that are as long as you want	Messages have to be no more than a sentence	Twitter

- What if this were being done in Japan?
- What if everything involved with your problem were 100 times smaller?
- What if it had to be done by tonight?
- What if you stopped trying to tackle it?
- What if you had to come up with *five* different workable solutions to your problem?
- What if the only things you could use to solve this problem were a hammer and some honey?

OLD IDEA + OLD IDEA = NEW IDEA

Few of us have truly original ideas, but we can easily come up with new ideas by combining old ones. All new ideas are, in a way, a re-combination of old patterns – yet that doesn't stop the result from being exciting. Music is a good example. Oasis, one of the most successful rock bands of modern times, drew heavily on ideas from The Beatles. The Beatles, in turn, were inspired by rock and roll, Indian music and medieval church music. Their talent was in combining these influences with modern lyrics and instruments.

You can come up with instant new ideas simply by mixing things that don't normally go together.

Let's imagine you need to come up with a new menu for a restaurant. The box opposite contains pairs of foods that are commonly combined with each other.

To create a new meal, pick one item from the left-hand column and one from a different row in the right-hand column.

Ice cream with curry sauce … pancakes with horseradish

MAIN FOOD	"NORMAL" PARTNER
Burgers	Barbecue sauce
Beef	Horseradish
Pork	Apple sauce
Chicken	Curry sauce
Bacon	Fried egg
Ice cream	Strawberries
Pancakes	Maple syrup

… beef and strawberries … burgers with maple syrup? That selection will certainly challenge the taste buds.

They might sound like a culinary nightmare, but perhaps that's just because you've never tried them. Can you see any new pairs that might actually work?

The Fat Duck restaurant in Bray, a village on the River Thames, has won three Michelin stars for its innovative meals and is one of the best restaurants in the world. The restaurant owner, Heston Blumenthal, is famous for combining foods that are normally kept apart. Among the delights that have been served there are bacon-and-egg ice cream, snail porridge and chocolate with tobacco.

"Nothing's really original. Not Homer or Shakespeare and certainly not you. Get over it."

Twyla Tharp, choreographer

PRODUCTS THAT COULD HAVE COME FROM "OLD COMBINATIONS" BRAINSTORMING		
OLD IDEA	**OLD IDEA**	**RESULT**
Digital clock	Bedside radio	Radio alarm clocks
Pocket camera	Cellphone	Smartphones
Multiple Choice quiz	Huge cash prize	*Who Wants to be a Millionaire?*
High school comedy	Vampire Horror	*Buffy the Vampire Slayer*
Plane	Helicopter	The V22 Osprey

DELIBERATELY RESTRICTING YOURSELF

Sometimes, the more freedom you have to express your ideas, the harder it can be to find inspiration.

ONE-MINUTE CHALLENGE – THINGS YOU CANNOT SEE

Find something to record your ideas, and then try this exercise:

Challenge 1: The unseen objects
Come up with a list of ten different objects that you can't currently see around you.

Challenge 2: Unseen objects beginning with "C"
Now repeat the first challenge, but this time think of ten objects beginning with "C" that you can't currently see.

In the one-minute challenge box above, the first challenge should have been easier – after all, you had just about every object on the planet available to you. Yet, bizarrely, there were probably moments when you were stuck. That almost infinite choice didn't help! You may well have found that you came up with a richer variety of ideas in the second challenge, where you were only allowed to think of objects beginning with "C". The constraint took some of the pressure off ("how could I possibly be expected to come up with ten ideas?") and also gave your mind something to focus on.

You can use this principle to help with your own creative challenge. If a project is too open-ended, you can be dazzled by the endless choice, and if you aren't careful you can find yourself flitting from one idea to the next. Imposing a rule or constraint on yourself helps to focus your ideas.

SOME FAMOUS "CONSTRAINED" CREATIONS

CURIOUS MUSIC

The book *The Curious Incident of the Dog in the Night-Time* was turned into an award-winning play. Part of its success was the music. The composer, Adrian Sutton, had the challenge of thinking of music that would be relevant to this play about a boy called Christopher who describes himself as "a mathematician with some behavioural difficulties". The composer was, in theory, free to come up with any music he wanted, but he found it helped to put a constraint on himself. The character Christopher is particularly fond of prime numbers (numbers that are only divisible by themselves and by 1). The first prime numbers are 2, 3, 5, 7, 11 and 13. So Adrian decided to base all of the music — the rhythm, the notes themselves, the

PUZZLE: WHAT IF? ... ADDING UP

Here's a puzzle about adding numbers. At first it might seem impossible — but it turns out there are several answers that are perfectly fair. If you find yourself stuck, allow yourself to ask some ridiculous "What if?" questions and see if they lead you to any solutions.

The numbers 1 to 9 have been written on cards and put into two columns. The column on the left adds to 24, and the column on the right adds to 21. Move one (and only one) card to make the two columns add to the same total. Can you find two different ways to do it?

4	1
5	2
6	3
9	7
	8

harmonies – on prime numbers. The audience may never have realized this, but the result was a score that won an Olivier Award.

A FILM WITH NO CUTS

In 1948, the film director Alfred Hitchcock forced a huge constraint on himself by deciding to create a thriller called *Rope* that was to take place in "real time". To make this convincing, he wanted the film to appear to have been recorded in one continuous shot with one camera. In practice that wasn't possible (a single roll of film could only do ten minutes), but he was able to disguise most of the cuts by doing a close-up on an object that faded into black.

ROUND BUILDING

The Capitol Tower in Hollywood, built in 1956, was the world's first circular office building. Capitol Records' business was selling records, so the inspiration for the look of the building was a simple, if radical, one: to build a tower that looked like a stack of records on a turntable. Today, office buildings with a circular cross-section have become commonplace throughout the world.

A RESTRICTED STORY

There are countless books in which a story is constrained by some feature. It might be a location, such as the beach in Thailand that inspired *The Beach*, or an object, such as the Vermeer painting that inspired *Girl with a Pearl Earring*. An extreme example is *La Dispurition*, a French novel by Georges Perec, in which he imposed on himself the constraint of never using the letter "e". This must have forced him to explore language and expression to the limits.

RANDOM WORDS

Perhaps the most off-the-wall way to spark your imagination is to deliberately add a completely unrelated word to your current thinking. The random word – which might be "badger", for example – takes your thinking in an unexpected direction. And because a badger, or whatever other random word you choose, was never meant to be a part of your idea it pretty much forces you to come up with ideas that will be "silly". As with the constraints mentioned elsewhere, introducing a random word takes away the stress of having to come up with a "good" idea. But it also guarantees you'll come up with something novel.

You can find a random word simply by opening a dictionary and choosing the first noun that you find. For example, if you're trying to think of uses for a dried-up ballpoint pen (remember the example on page 16), you might randomly pick the word "hairstyle" from the dictionary. How can you link "hairstyle" to using a dried-up pen?

Perhaps you could do it in the following ways:

- Use the pen as a hair curler.
- Cut the pen up into small hoops and use them as hair beads.
- Use the shaft of the pen to store strands of hair (or other long, thin things).
- Use the pen to comb out tangles.

These four ideas weren't in the original list of possible uses, and you can probably think of more. I've tried the inkless ballpoint pen challenge on two groups. The first group has to come up with any ideas, the second has to come up with ideas linked to a random word they were given. The average score of the group given the random word is often higher.

USING THE RANDOM-WORD METHOD

With practise, the random-word technique can be used in just about any situation, from inventing a new product to re-thinking the best way to collect taxes. On page 131 you'll find a small selection of words to get you started. Follow this simple step-by-step process and see what comes out of it:

1. **Decide on the problem you are looking for ideas for**
    Let's say the challenge is to come up with ideas for a venue for a 40th birthday party

2. **Pick a number at random between 1 and 60**
    To make it truly random, look at your watch or clock and check the number of seconds past the minute at the instant you look. If it's 16 seconds past the minute, go with the number 16.

3. **Look at the random word list**
    Find the number you've chosen, and look at the word beside it. However inappropriate the word might seem, this is the one that you'll be combining with your idea.

4. **Incorporate that word into your problem**
    Word number 16 is "Umbrella". Re-define the challenge

as: "Come up with ideas for a 40th birthday venue linked to 'umbrellas'."

5. **List things that you associate with the random word**
   For example, for "Umbrella", you might think of: wet weather, umbrella stands, paintings in which umbrellas appear, umbrellas as walking sticks, Gene Kelly in *Singin' in the Rain*.

6. **Let the ideas flow**
   For example: "Go somewhere that requires an umbrella, such as a tropical rainforest ... or a place nearer to home that has an artificial rainforest (botanical gardens), or a theme park with water rides, or a trip out on a yacht ... Taking a different path, what about a place where you find umbrellas – an old hotel where they still have umbrella stands? – have a party at a grand hotel ... or the Lost Property department of a big station, for example Paddington – go on a special steam train outing."

"If you want to tell people the truth, you'd better make them laugh, otherwise they'll kill you."

George Bernard Shaw

RANDOM WORD LIST

1	Rabbit	21	Concrete	41	Gravestone
2	Tooth	22	Snowball	42	Robin
3	Yoga	23	Fireplace	43	Smoke
4	Suitcase	24	Nail polish	44	Trombone
5	Budgerigar	25	Calculator	45	Cat food
6	Crystals	26	Syringe	46	Ladder
7	Nail-clippers	27	Broccoli	47	Opera
8	Basketball	28	Swing	48	Fencing
9	Feathers	29	Seatbelt	49	Drainpipes
10	Goat	30	Top hat	50	Cave
11	Nun	31	Toenails	51	Seagull
12	Cliffs	32	Gold	52	Oxygen
13	Hammer	33	Cherry tree	53	Astronaut
14	Camera	34	Chocolate	54	Vikings
15	Bacon	35	Quiz show	55	Rodeo
16	Umbrella	36	Violin	56	Whispers
17	Bow tie	37	Shampoo	57	X-ray
18	Maple leaf	38	Iceberg	58	Apple
19	Barbed wire	39	Kennel	59	Helicopter
20	Taxicab	40	Pyjamas	60	Mackerel

PUZZLE: BREAKING OUT AGAIN

In the nine-dot puzzle on page 33 of this book, you were set
the challenge of finding a way to connect all the dots using
only four straight lines, without your pen leaving the paper.
In fact, it's possible to solve this puzzle using fewer than four
straight lines — and there's more than one way of doing it with
only one. Can you find them, without breaking the rules?

MESSY CREATIVITY 4:
POST-IT® NOTES

Today, Post-it® notes are a familiar sight in our offices and homes. It seems incredible that something so useful took so long to appear.

In 1968, Spencer Silver, a chemist working for the 3M corporation, discovered a very weak adhesive. Searching for a use for this product, 3M developed the Post-it® bulletin board, which had a sticky surface so that people didn't need to use thumb-tacks. It was not a success.

The next idea came from Art Fry, a researcher at 3M. Sitting in church one day, he got frustrated that the bits of paper he was using as bookmarks in a hymnal kept slipping out, and had the idea for slightly sticky bookmarks, using the 3M glue. He tested the idea at work, but there was little demand. Some time later, Fry had his second flash of inspiration – to scribble a message on a sticky note and fix it to a document. Now the idea became popular. Even so, he met resistance from the company and a lack of interest from the public. However, so many people at 3M believed this idea was good that they gave it another launch in 1980, this time as the Post-it® note.

The same themes occur time and again: the value of many ideas is recognized only after the event, and the creative process can be arduous and filled with uncertainty. If that's how your project feels, then take heart – you could still be on to something big.

12
TAKING IDEAS FORWARD

The buzz you get after you've had an idea can quickly disappear. Ideas that seemed so exciting today can seem flawed and impractical when you think about them again tomorrow morning. And six months later when somebody asks: "Whatever happened about that idea of yours…" the answer will often be "Nothing ever came of it."

So, whether you're developing ideas on your own or with others, what does it take to turn ideas into more than just stimulating thoughts?

EVALUATE!

On page 103 I mentioned how creative problem-solving can be done in three stages: define the Problem, then generate Ideas, then Evaluate the ideas (that's P-I-E for short).

When you've finished generating ideas (this might have been a formal brainstorming or just some idle jottings) you can do some evaluation straight away. In particular, try to pick out the ideas that seem to have most potential.

If more than one of you will be taking the ideas forward then it's important to select ideas that you both support. A simple vote is often the way to pick out the best ideas quickly. The most popular two or three ideas should then be evaluated in more depth.

The simplest way to evaluate an idea is to look at it in two ways: what are its advantages?, and what are its drawbacks? But there are other, more in-depth ways to evaluate ideas.

Edward de Bono, the lateral-thinking guru, developed a method called *Six Thinking Hats* in which there are six (imaginary) coloured hats to represent different ways of thinking about an idea, including the yellow hat (what's good about the idea?) and the black hat (what's wrong with it?). A simpler version is called PMI, which stands for Plus-Minus-Interesting. In other words, when evaluating an idea, list what you think are its Plus-points, its Minus-points, but also what are its Interesting points. An interesting idea may not immediately be workable, but it might be the starting point for a far better idea somewhere down the line.

Alternatively, you can do what's known as a NAF Rating, a method of rating ideas that belongs to a problem-solving approach known as "Synectics", first developed in the 1950s.

The NAF Rating rates an idea on three measures: Novelty, Appeal and Feasibility.

What's nice about this little technique is that it recognizes that ideas can have different qualities. Buying Aunt Mabel a cookery book for Christmas may be feasible and fairly appealing (to her) but it's not exactly novel. Treating her to a trip to a theme park, on the other hand, would score high on novelty, but may score lower on appeal and feasibility.

But instant evaluation isn't always the best way to judge the quality of an idea. For this reason, you should try to avoid throwing away ideas that don't immediately pass the test. Keep a record of all the ideas you had, because what looks good today may not look so good tomorrow, and vice versa. "Sleeping on it" allows your subconscious to process the details of ideas, and is one of the best ways of ensuring that you have come up with ideas that are worth pursuing.

TURNING DRAWBACKS INTO PROBLEMS TO SOLVE

One of the reasons why ideas don't get acted upon is that they turn out to have drawbacks. The solution you thought would work turns out to be too expensive; or people you thought would like it turn out to not be in favour.

Instead of letting these drawbacks be permanent blocks for an idea, you can treat the negatives as problems to solve, just like the "Three Positives" approach described on page 82. The idea is too expensive? – How can you find a cheaper version? The customer didn't like the idea when you tried it out? – What would need to change in the idea for it to be more appealing?

In fact you can think of the P-I-E model of creative problem-solving as being a cycle: once you've had ideas and evaluated them, if the ideas aren't perfect then those imperfections are a problem that you need to "solve".

This means you are just going through the P-I-E in a loop, refining the ideas each time.

What this demonstrates is that ideas evolve, just as they did with the roof of Sydney Opera House (page 71) and the lyrics to the songs in Evita (page 115). Very often the crude idea you had at the start turns into something very different when you finally implement it. That doesn't make the original idea bad or wrong, and it might be more helpful instead to think of early ideas as being like a first draft, or the first rung on the ladder.

PLANNING FOR THE WORST CASE

Just as it's important to look at the plus side of ideas that have drawbacks, it's also vital to take a realistic look at the possible downsides of an idea that at first seems brilliant. What if it goes wrong? What's the worst that could happen? If you set out all the things that might go wrong, you can begin to plan for them and think how to minimize their impact. By thinking about these potential problems early on, you'll pre-empt some of the snags that could otherwise crop up later.

For risky ideas, think about what you can do to reduce the risk. For example, if you can't face the prospect of giving up your job to take on a new, risky venture, is it possible to start the project in your spare time or when you're on leave? Or could you negotiate some "time out"? This is why considering a plan B from the start (page 113) can be particularly helpful.

ACTION PLANS AND DEADLINES

Nothing beats a deadline for forcing you to act on an idea.
If you have a presentation to give next week, then however
negative you feel about the ideas you have at the moment,
you'll definitely have to do *something* before the big day.

You might think that pressure stifles creative thinking,
and sometimes this is true – under too much stress, you can
panic and the mind goes blank. But more often a deadline
helps to get the creative juices going. If you know you have
to deliver, you've no choice but to let some of your raw ideas
get through (as the Indian restaurant example on page 112
demonstrated).

Without the constraint of a deadline, however, you have
time to think of a hundred reasons why your idea won't
work. To encourage you to act on an idea, here are a couple
of tips.

Set your own deadline – if acting on your idea doesn't
already have a deadline, set yourself one. If it's part of a big
project, break it down into a series of milestones. When you
get to each milestone, you can reflect on how you're doing
and how to tackle the next step.

Promise others you'll do it – if you want to be sure
that you'll complete a task, raise the stakes by making a
commitment to other people. The more publicly you make
that commitment, the harder it is to back out without
losing face.

BEATING THE MID-PROJECT BLUES

I once met an architect who designed sports stadia. It sounded like a dream job, and he agreed that it definitely had its exciting and glamorous moments. But he said that usually the best parts of a project were the beginning (the flash of inspiration when he first had the idea) and the end (seeing the idea completed).

In the middle, he'd run into what he called the "mid-project blues".

The excitement of beginning, and the euphoria at the end, can seem very far away when you're halfway through and you've hit a problem. At these moments, it's common to find yourself thinking:

- "Why am I doing this?"
- "Are we going down a blind alley here?"
- "Is the idea really that good?"

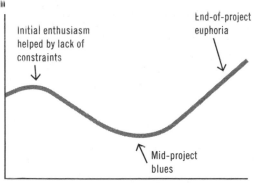

Anyone who has worked on an idea that took a lot of time and effort to implement has probably experienced these emotions at some point.

If you've nothing to spur you on except your pride, this can be a dangerous phase for an idea. If you do encounter the mid-project blues, these tips may be helpful:

- Remember you are not alone: mid-project blues are almost a rite of passage for big ideas.
- Take a break, to give yourself a chance to refresh your thinking.
- Remind yourself why you started acting on this idea in the first place – why you thought it was good, what you thought the difficulties would be and what other people liked about it.
- Review where you've got to so far by involving somebody with a positive attitude, and have another round of brainstorming just to give yourself a dose of the feel-good factor.

"A man with a new idea is a crank until the idea succeeds."

Mark Twain

SOME FINAL THOUGHTS

All of the approaches and techniques I've described in this book are ones that I've used myself. But if I had to extract the most basic principles that apply every day to nearly every human interaction, they are these:

- Creativity is an essential part of what makes us human, and ideas are the basis of creativity. But ideas are fragile, and easily killed. And unfortunately …

- It is human nature to see the disadvantages in any idea, and to want to point them out. This is fine, except that this tendency for our first reaction to be negative kills off ideas that have the potential to be valuable.

- You can help ideas to flourish by making it safe for you and for others to put forward ideas without fear of them being criticized – by setting the rules in advance, and by encouraging an attitude in which you see the positives first.

- Whenever you're stuck – and even sometimes when you aren't – step back and ask, "Why is this a problem?" and "What is stopping me from solving it?" That's often all you need to inspire you to "Aha!" moments of lateral thinking.

Finally, it's worth remembering that the people who tend to be most creative and open to new ideas are children.

Perhaps the most important message of this book is therefore that, when it comes to thinking creatively, it helps to recapture the best aspects of child-like behaviour.

And if that means occasionally allowing yourself to tolerate a bit more silliness … well maybe that's not such a bad idea.

SOLUTIONS

CHAPTER 1
PAGE 16 ONE-MINUTE CHALLENGE: THE INKLESS BALLPOINT PEN
Possible uses for the inkless pen include: blowpipe, storage
case for pins, whisky measure, model of a pen, quill,
thermometer holder, seed dibber, lever, back-scratcher,
toothpick, puncture repair tool, keyboard cleaner, pipette,
whistle, catapult, door wedge, prop for a stage play, comb,
stirrer, ring holder, knob at the end of a light cord, slider to
run along a string, screwdriver, mashing device, insulator,
conductor's baton, fishing rod, drumstick, drinking straw,
wedge to prop open a window, sweetcorn holder, fine
paintbrush handle, hole puncher, spring (use the bendy ink
cartridge), roller for fine pastry.

CHAPTER 2
PAGE 32 PUZZLE: JOINING THE DOTS
This is the classic four-line solution for the nine-dot puzzle.

CHAPTER 3
PAGE 43 PUZZLE: CAN YOU THINK LIKE A CHILD?
When a class of ten-year-old children is given this puzzle,
here are the solutions that they come up with most often:
• Put the trees on islands and dig around them.

- Make the pool twice as deep.
- Build a new square swimming pool somewhere else.

The lateral thinking in that last answer really appeals to me.

However, there is another solution that children don't come up with very often, and it's the one that the Robinson family actually adopted. If you rotate the square by 45 degrees you can increase it to twice the size and still fit it between the trees.

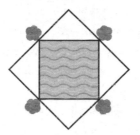

While the children's other solutions are wonderfully creative, they usually think the diamond solution is the best.

PAGE 47 PUZZLES: THREE LATERAL-THINKING QUICKIES

Question 1: Canadians (like everyone else) eat less in February for the simple reason that there are fewer days than in any other month.

Question 2: Today is 1 January, and Sally's birthday is 31 December. Two days ago she was still 12, yesterday was her 13th birthday, at the end of this year she'll be 14, and at the end of next year she'll be 15.

Question 3: E. The sequence consists of the initial letters of the number sequence "One", "Two", "Three", "Four" and so on.

CHAPTER 4

PAGE 61 PUZZLE: A SURPRISE IN THE MIRROR

Most people "know" that the answer is (a), that you can see more of yourself when you step back from a mirror – but it turns out that most people are wrong.

The answer is, in fact, (b): as you step back from the mirror, you can still only see down to your navel. I wouldn't be surprised if you don't believe me, and rush off to find the nearest mirror to test this out.

Why do people get this wrong?

Probably because mirrors are often tilted downward slightly, so when you step back from them you do see more of yourself. When you're confronted by a new problem, it's natural to look for similarities to situations that you've encountered before. But although the problem you're facing now might look the same as certain aspects of your past experience, perhaps it's subtly different in some way. Your existing knowledge can sometimes mislead you.

CHAPTER 8

PAGE 99 PUZZLE: THE DICTIONARY BOOKMARKS

The most common answer offered is that the bookmarks are 10cm apart (the thickness of the two books).

The correct answer, however, is less than 1cm. To see why, imagine taking the first volume off the shelf and opening it at the first page. (If you find picturing this difficult, do it with a real book). Now place the book back on the shelf again. The first page is on the *right* of the first volume, not the left, and that is roughly where the Aardvark entry will be. Meanwhile Zebra, which is near the last page of the second volume, will be on the left.

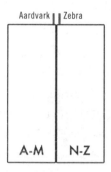

Aardvark | Zebra

A-M | N-Z

Like the puzzle with the bathroom mirror, the surprising thing here is how a real-world physical problem can have such an unexpected answer.

CHAPTER 11
PAGE 120 CHALLENGE. TRY THE OPPOSITES TECHNIQUE

Problem 1: Instead of "How to send Christmas cards in time" how about "How to send Christmas cards late". This suggests the idea of sending New Year cards instead. It's not such a silly idea: people don't have time to read all their cards and letters before Christmas anyway, so your communication might have more impact if you delay it. (Another approach would be: "How to NOT send Christmas cards at all" – emailing a card has become a common eco-friendly (or lazy, some people say) solution to the card-sending problem.

Problem 2: Instead of wondering how you can get the kids to school think about how to get them to get *you* to school.

What could this mean? You could take it literally – get them to hook a trailer onto their bikes and tow you. But there are more practical ways to interpret the challenge. Maybe, instead of chasing around to get the kids ready, you could put them in charge in the mornings. They have to complete everything on a checklist before they earn the right to a bit of pre-school TV (or whatever).

Problem 3: Instead of "How to encourage health and safety in the workplace" what about a training course encouraging sloppiness and risk. That wouldn't get past the corporate censors – but a training course looking at risk, and how far you can push the limits before you incur a hazard, would be more engaging than the regular worthy courses.

PAGE 126 PUZZLE: WHAT IF? ... ADDING UP

There's no solution if you just move one number to the other column, or if you remove one card altogether. So the solutions are going to have to be more devious.

Nobody said you can't turn cards around. What if you turn the 9 card around so it becomes a "6", and both columns now add up to 21.

4	1
5	2
6	3
9	7
	8

How else can you move only one card without cheating? What if you move one card on top of another. Take the 5 card and place it on top of the 7, so that 7 is hidden. Now both columns add to 19.

Similarly, you can put the 1 on top of the 5 (both columns now add to 20). Or place the 3 on the 9 (the totals are now 18).

But there's more. What if you flip a card over (its reverse is presumably blank). That opens up these solutions:

- Flip over the 3 and place it on top of the 6, so that both numbers are hidden. Both columns now add to 18.
- Likewise take the 6 and put it on top of the 3, again both add to 18.
- Or place the 1 upside down on the 4 – or vice versa – to get totals of 20.
- Or place the 2 upside down on the 5 or vice versa (totals 19).

If you are happy using maths notation, move the 2 bottom left of the 3, to make 2^3, which means $2 \times 2 \times 2$ (= 8) so both columns now add to 24.

Meanwhile, there is nothing in the rules that say you can't get ANOTHER unused card, write 3 on it and put that card in the second column so that both add to 24.

Or, if you want to get very literal in the way you read the wording: move 1 by picking it up and putting it back again, now the two columns are the same (as they were at the start).

Here are some more solutions to the nine-dot puzzle, taking you even further "out of the box".

Nine dots in three lines
If the dots are large enough, or the lines long and thin enough, this zig-zag solution will work. (Did you assume that the lines always had to go through the middle of the dots?)

Nine dots in one line
With a fat enough pen, all you need is one thick line.

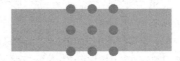

Other solutions include taping the paper around a tin can and drawing a diagonal line, or folding the paper and jamming the pen through the middle (some people regard this solution as cheating; others think it is a perfectly fair way of challenging the assumptions).

FURTHER READING

Rob Eastaway, *How Many Socks Make a Pair?*, Aurum Press, 2014

Betty Edwards, *Drawing on the Right Side of the Brain*, Souvenir Press, 2013

Richard Feynman, *What Do You Care What Other People Think?*, Penguin, 2007

Tim Harford, *Adapt: Why Success Always Starts with Failure*, Abacus, 2012

Keith Johnstone, *Impro: Improvisation in the Theatre*, Methuen Drama, 2007

Arthur Koestler, *The Act of Creation*, Penguin Arkana, 1989

Vincent Nolan, *The Innovator's Handbook*, Sphere, 1987

Dennis Sherwood, *Creating an Innovative Culture*, Capstone, 1998

Twyla Tharp, *The Creative Habit*, Simon & Schuster, 2007

INDEX

WATKINS

Sharing Wisdom Since
1893

The story of Watkins dates back to 1893, when the scholar of esotericism John Watkins founded a bookshop, inspired by the lament of his friend and teacher Madame Blavatsky that there was nowhere in London to buy books on mysticism, occultism or metaphysics. That moment marked the birth of Watkins, soon to become the home of many of the leading lights of spiritual literature, including Carl Jung, Rudolf Steiner, Alice Bailey and Chögyam Trungpa.

Today, the passion at Watkins Publishing for vigorous questioning is still resolute. Our wide-ranging and stimulating list reflects the development of spiritual thinking and new science over the past 120 years. We remain at the cutting edge, committed to publishing books that change lives.

DISCOVER MORE . . .

Read our blog

Watch and listen to
our authors in action

Sign up to
our mailing list

JOIN IN THE CONVERSATION

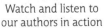 WatkinsPublishing    @watkinswisdom

 watkinsbooks    watkinswisdom   watkins-media

Our books celebrate conscious, passionate, wise and happy living.
Be part of the community by visiting

www.watkinspublishing.com